The Nation's #1 Educational P

The McGraw·Hill Companies

Preschool

Math

Numbers & Counting • Patterns
Classifying • Comparing

A McGraw·Hill/Warner Bros. Workbook

Table of Contents

Table of Contents (continued)

Credits:
McGraw-Hill Learning Materials Editorial/Production Team
Vincent F. Douglas, B.S. and M. Ed.
Tracy R. Paulus
Jennifer P. Blashkiw

Design Studio
Mike Legendre; Creativity On Demand

Warner Bros. Worldwide Publishing Editorial/ProductionTeam
Michael Harkavy
Charles Carney
Paula Allen
Allen Helbig
Victoria Selover

Illustrators
Cover: Renegade Animation
Interior: Ryan Dunlavey; Darryl Goudreau

McGraw-Hill
Consumer Products

A Division of The ***McGraw-Hill*** *Companies*

Published by McGraw-Hill Learning Materials, an imprint of McGraw-Hill Consumer Products.

Send all inquiries to:
McGraw-Hill Learning Materials
250 Old Wilson Bridge Road
Worthington, Ohio 43085

1-57768-209-2

NAME

ONE AND TWO

2	1
1	2
2	1

Directions: Following the example in the first box, have your child draw scoops of ice cream on each cone to show how many. Then ask your child to color the cones with 1 scoop brown and the cones with 2 scoops red. ***Skill:*** Identifying one and two.

NAME

WRITING 1 AND 2

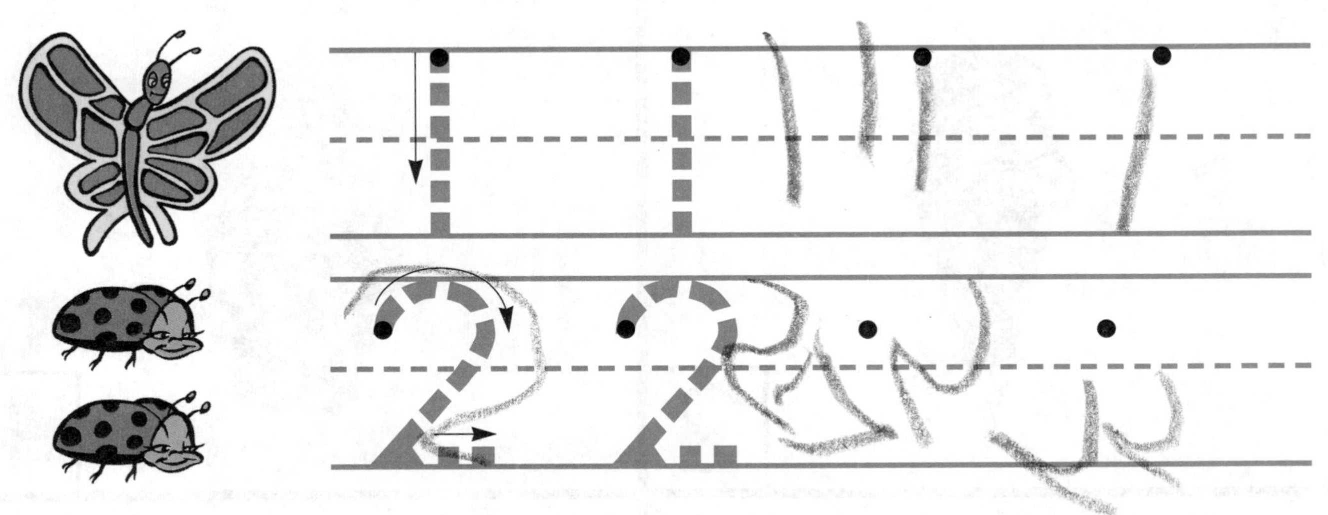

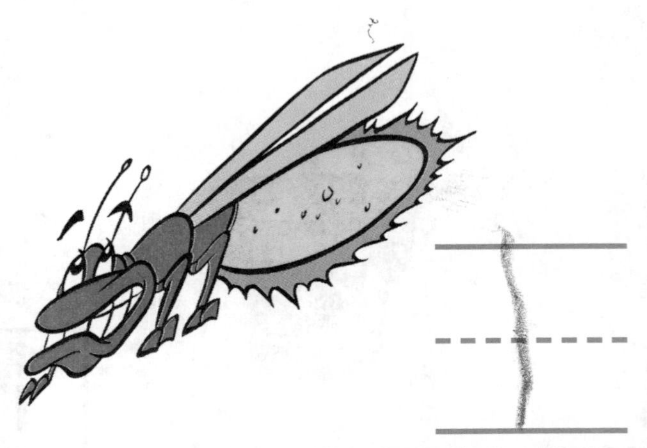

Directions: Have your child trace, then write the numbers 1 and 2 in the space provided at the top of the page. Ask your child to count the insects in each block, then write 1 or 2 to tell how many. ***Skill:*** Identifying and writing 1 and 2.

NAME ____________

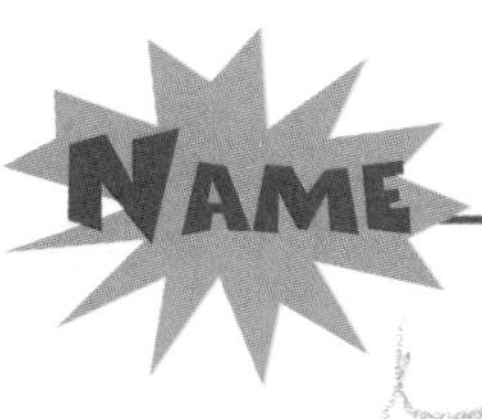

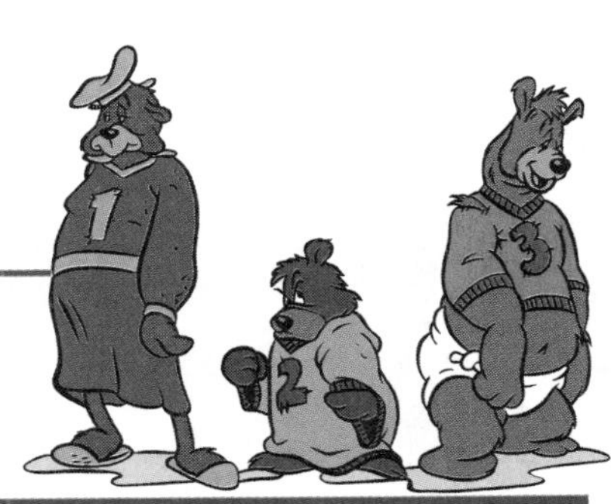

THREE

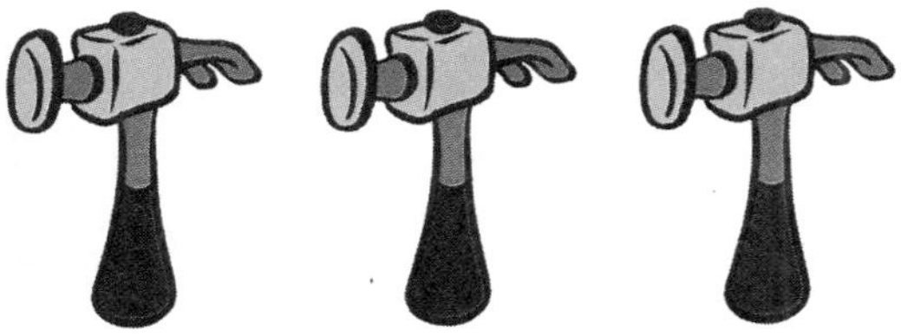

1 2 3

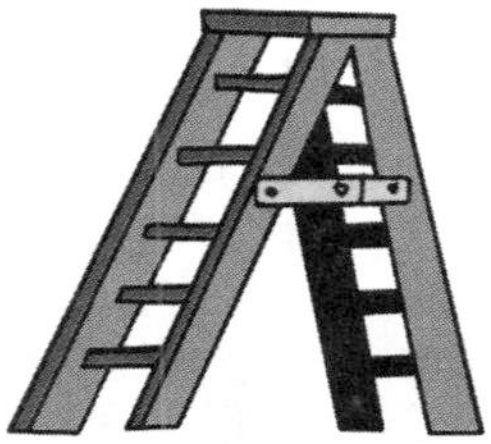

1 2 3

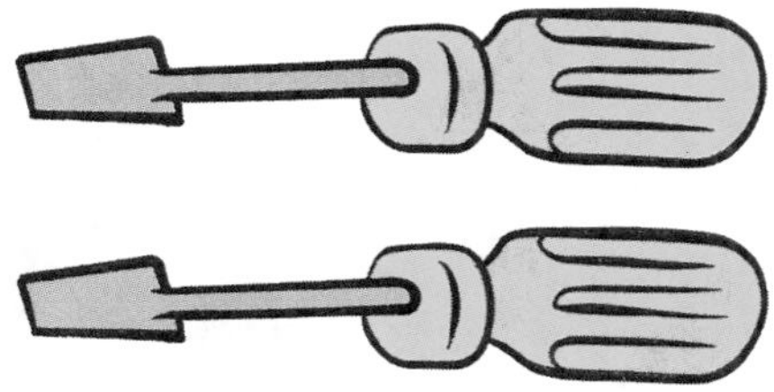

1 2 3

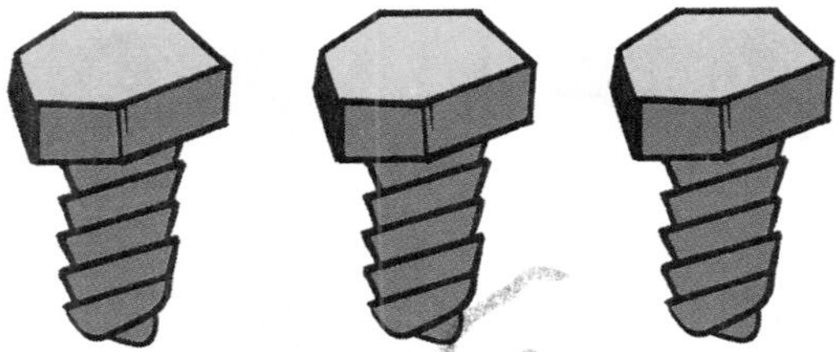

1 2 3

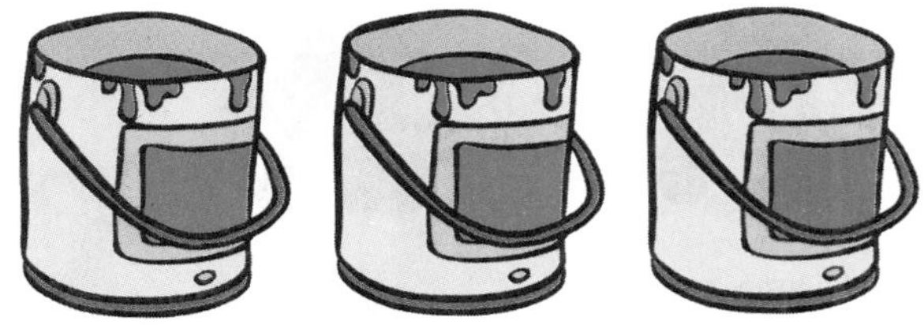

1 2 3

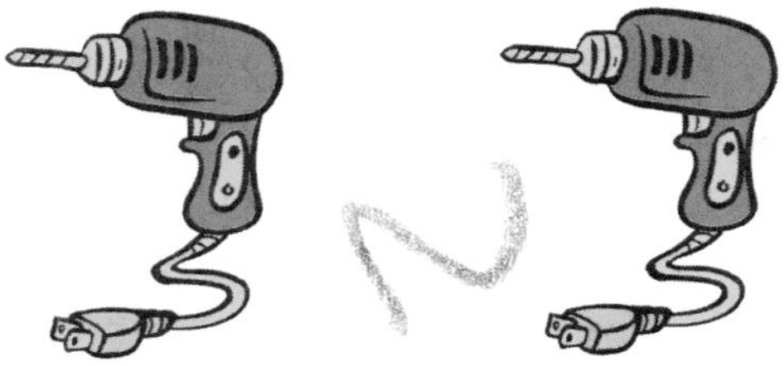

1 2 3

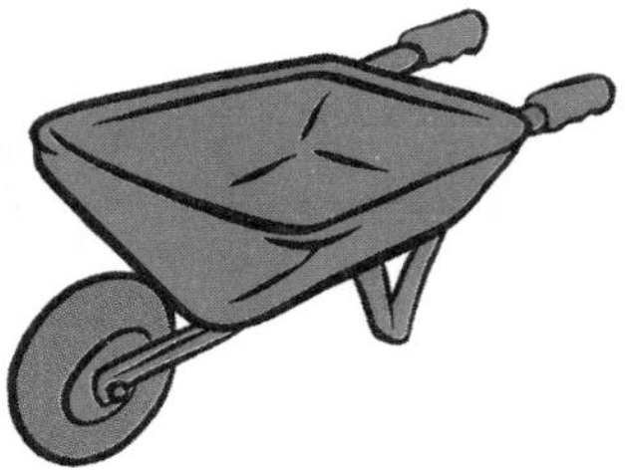

1 2 3

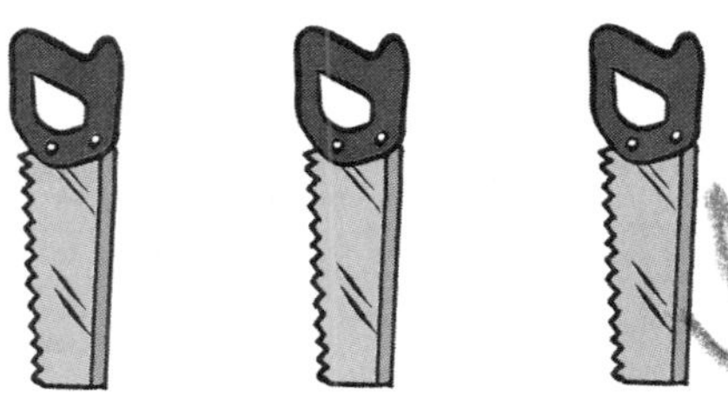

1 2 3

Directions: Have your child count the objects in each block, then circle the correct number to show how many. ***Skill:*** Identifying groups of one to three.

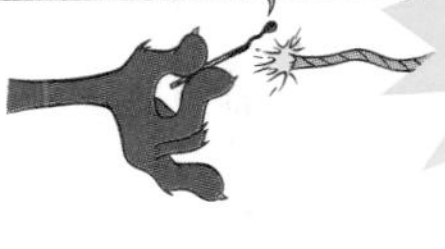

NAME

FOUR

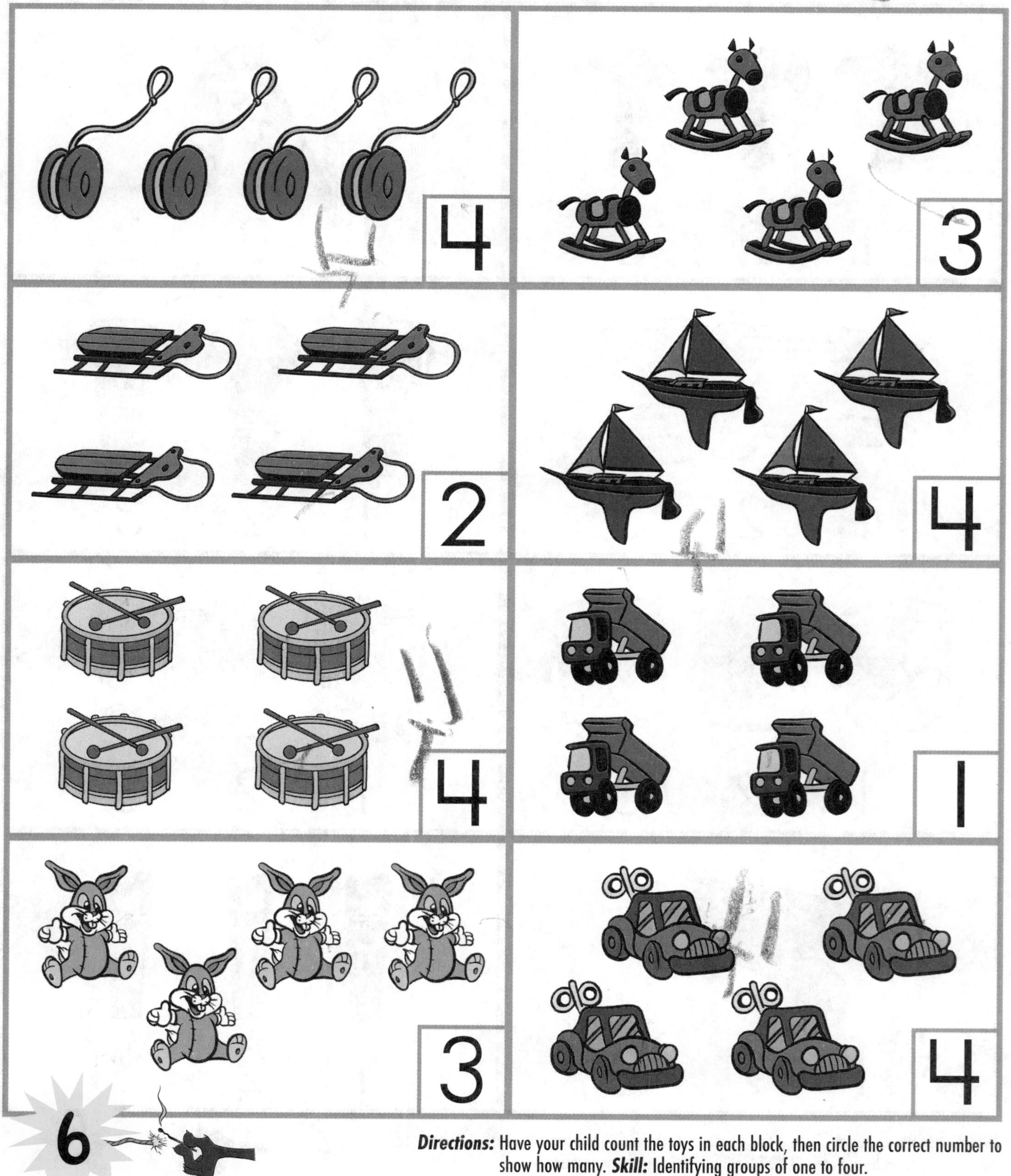

4	3
2	4
4	1
3	4

Directions: Have your child count the toys in each block, then circle the correct number to show how many. ***Skill:*** Identifying groups of one to four.

WRITING 3 AND 4

3 3

4 4

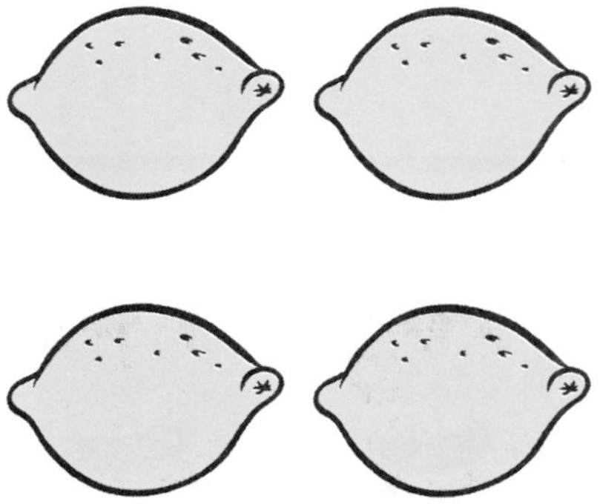

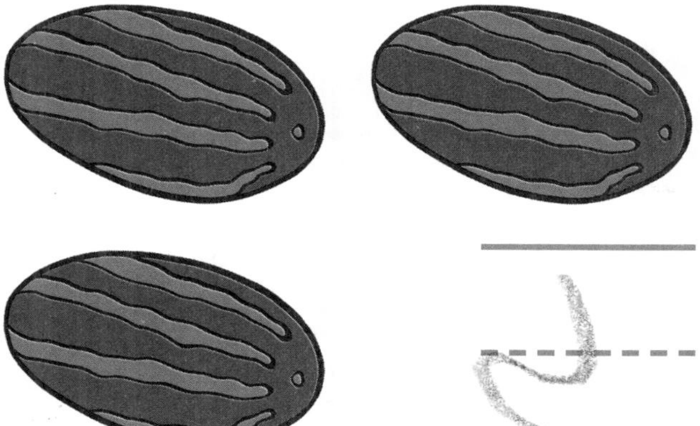

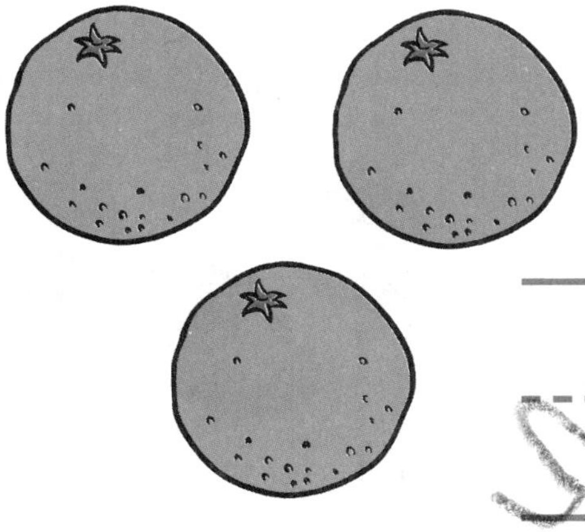

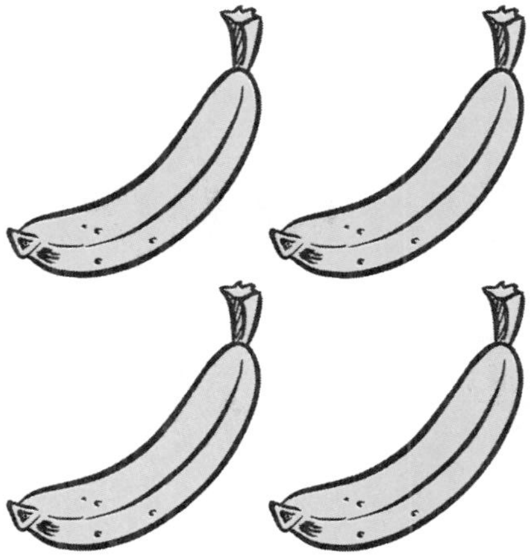

Directions: Have your child trace, then write the numbers 3 and 4 in the space provided at the top of the page. Ask your child to count the pieces of fruit in each block, then write 3 or 4 to tell how many. ***Skill:*** Identifying and writing 3 and 4.

NAME

FIVE

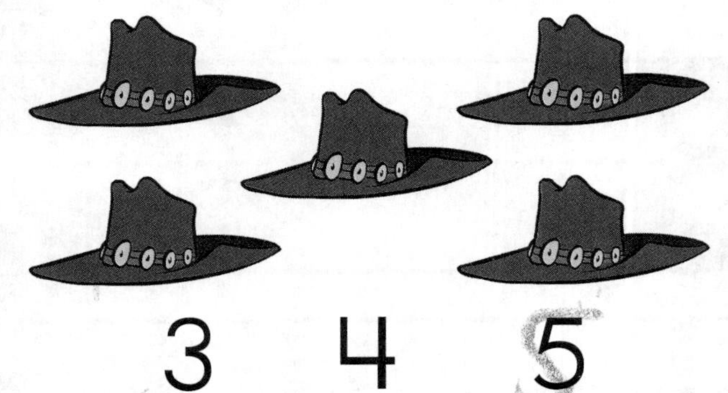

3 4 5

2 3 4

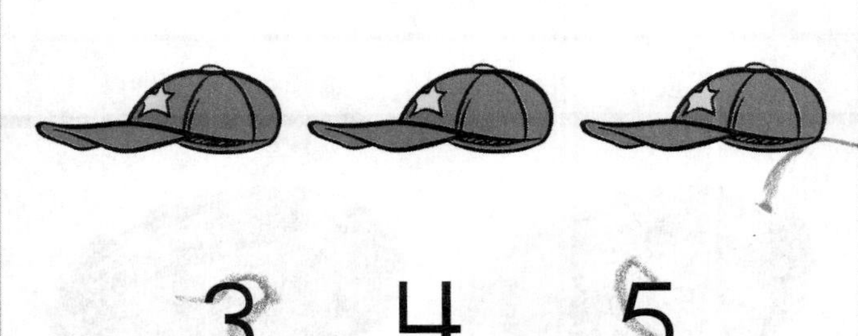

3 4 5

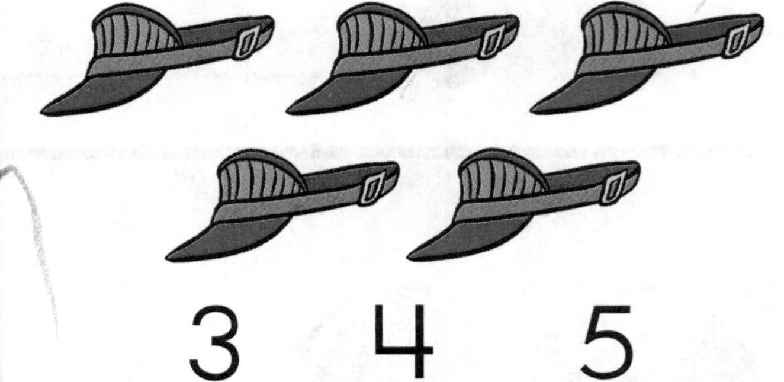

3 4 5

1 2 3

3 4 5

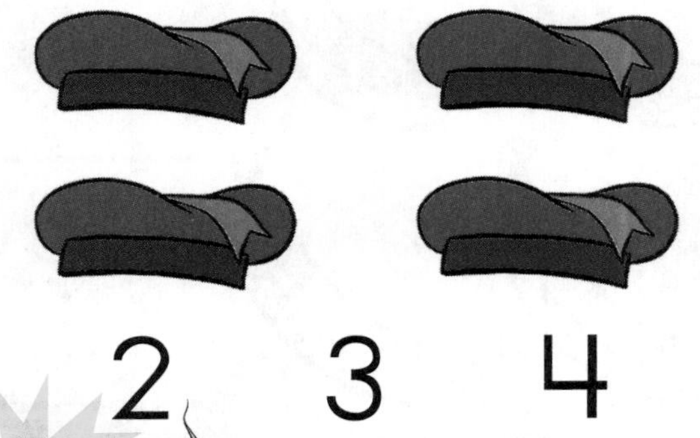

2 3 4

3 4 5

Directions: Have your child count the hats in each block, then circle the correct number to show how many. ***Skill:*** Identifying groups of one to five.

4	
2	
0	
5	
1	
3	

Directions: Have your child look at the numbers at the beginning of each row, then circle the correct number of flowers to show how many. ***Skill:*** Identifying groups of zero to five.

NAME ______________________

WRITING 5 AND 0

5

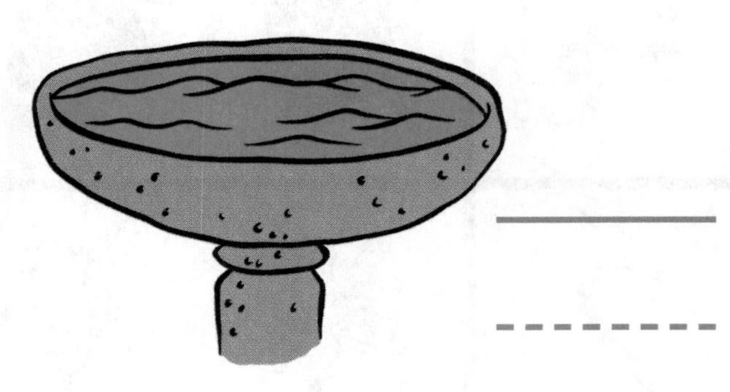

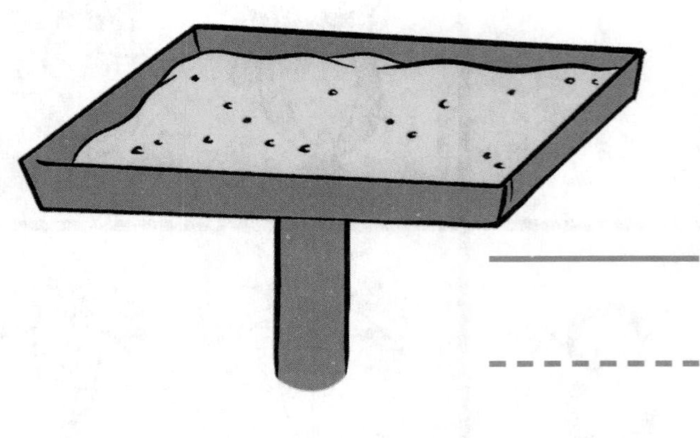

Directions: Have your child count the birds in each block, then write 5 or 0 to tell how many.
Skill: Identifying and writing 5 and 0.

NAME ______________________________

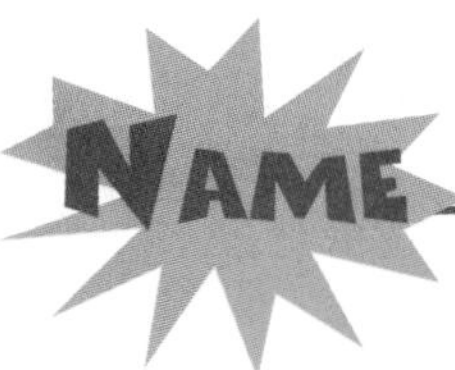

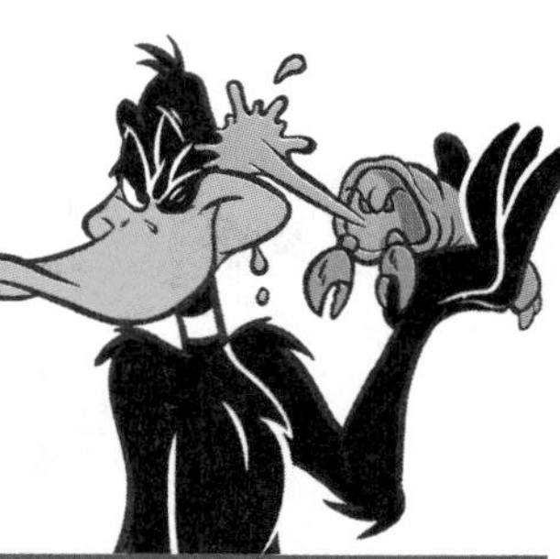

ORDER 0 TO 5

0	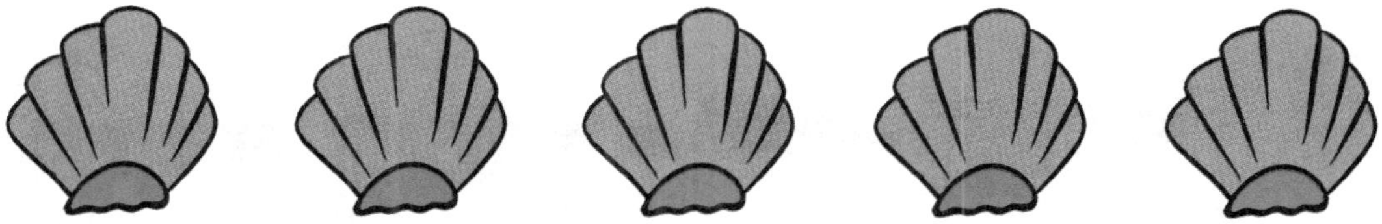
1	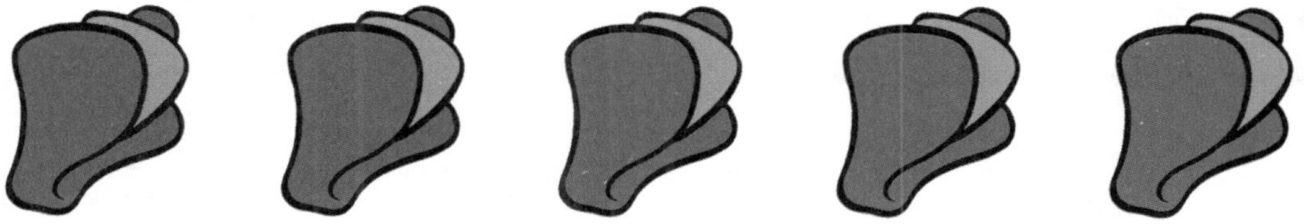
2	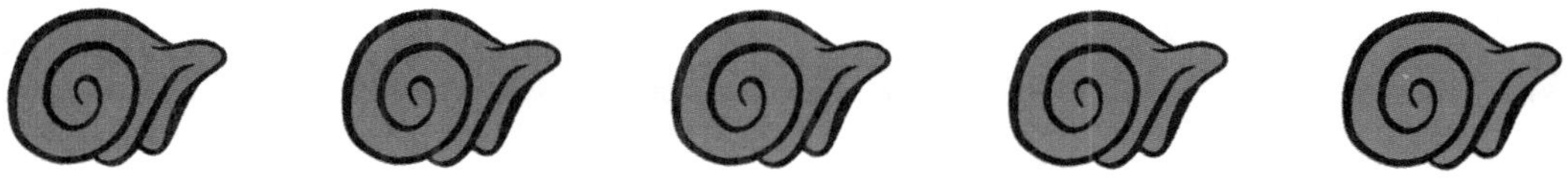
3	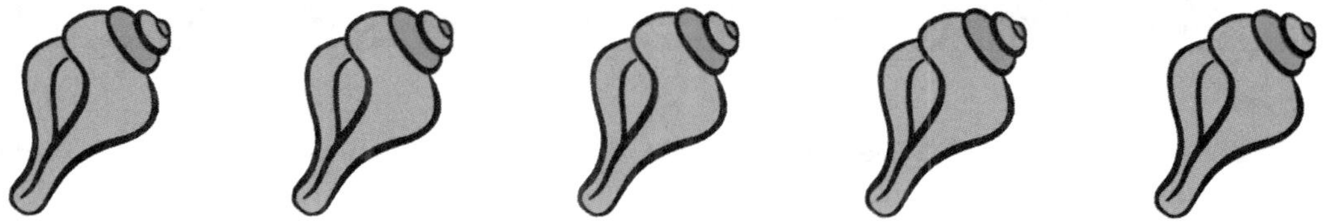
4	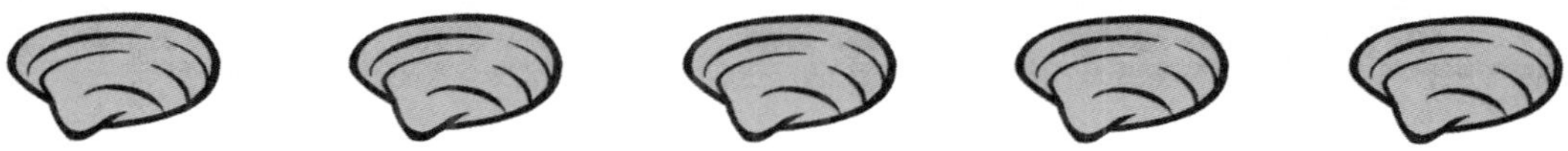
5	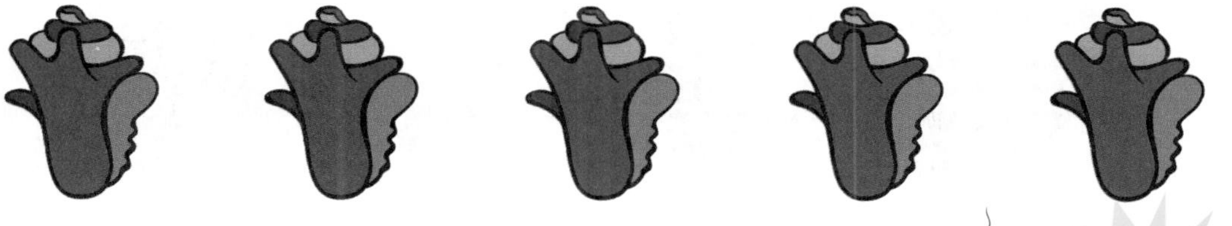

Directions: Have your child trace the numbers at the beginning of each row, then circle the correct number of shells to show how many. ***Skill:*** Identifying number order from 0 to 5.

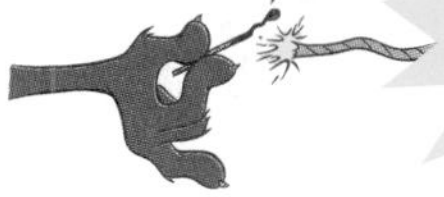

NAME ______________________________

ORDINALS TO FIFTH

Directions: Have your child circle the first car in the first row, the second car in the second row, and continue this pattern to the fifth row. ***Skill:*** Identifying ordinal positions first to fifth.

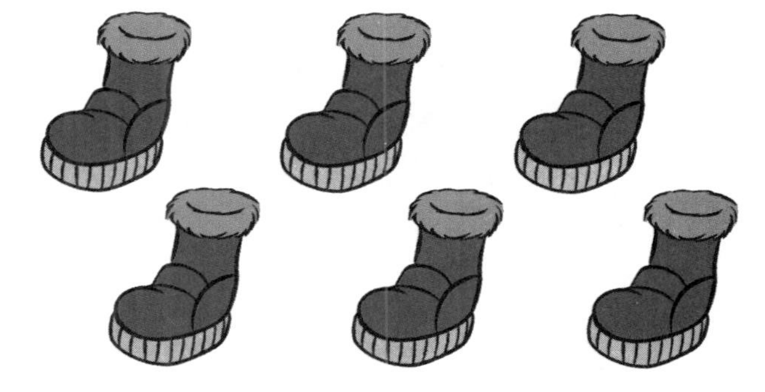

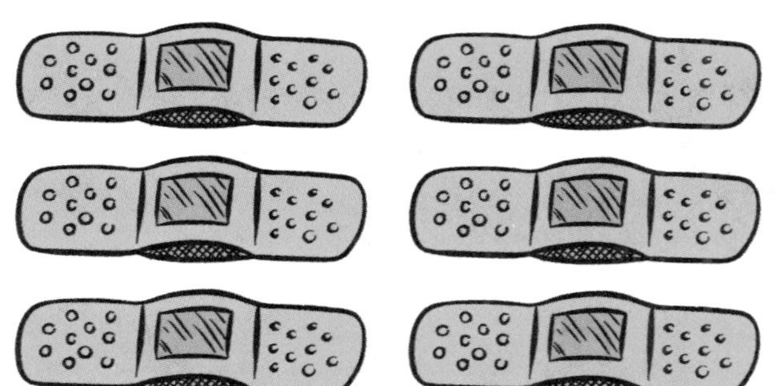

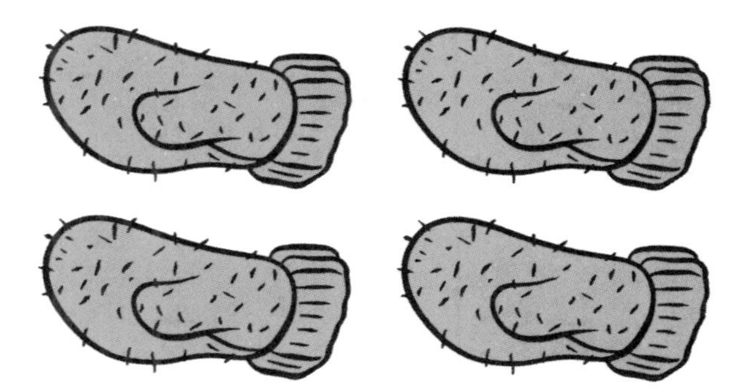

Directions: Have your child count the objects in each group, then circle the group if it shows 6.
Skill: Identifying groups of six.

NAME ______________________________

SEVEN

2 3 4	5 6 7
5 6 7	1 2 3
5 6 7	5 6 7
5 6 7	5 6 7

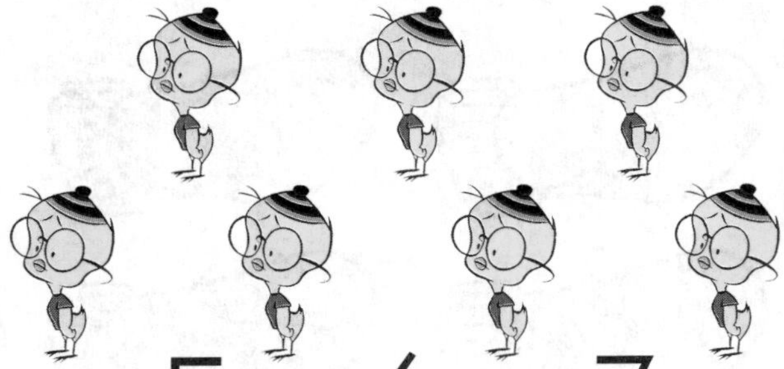

Directions: Have your child count the birds in each block, then circle the correct number to show how many. ***Skill:*** Identifying groups of one to seven.

WRITING 6 AND 7

7

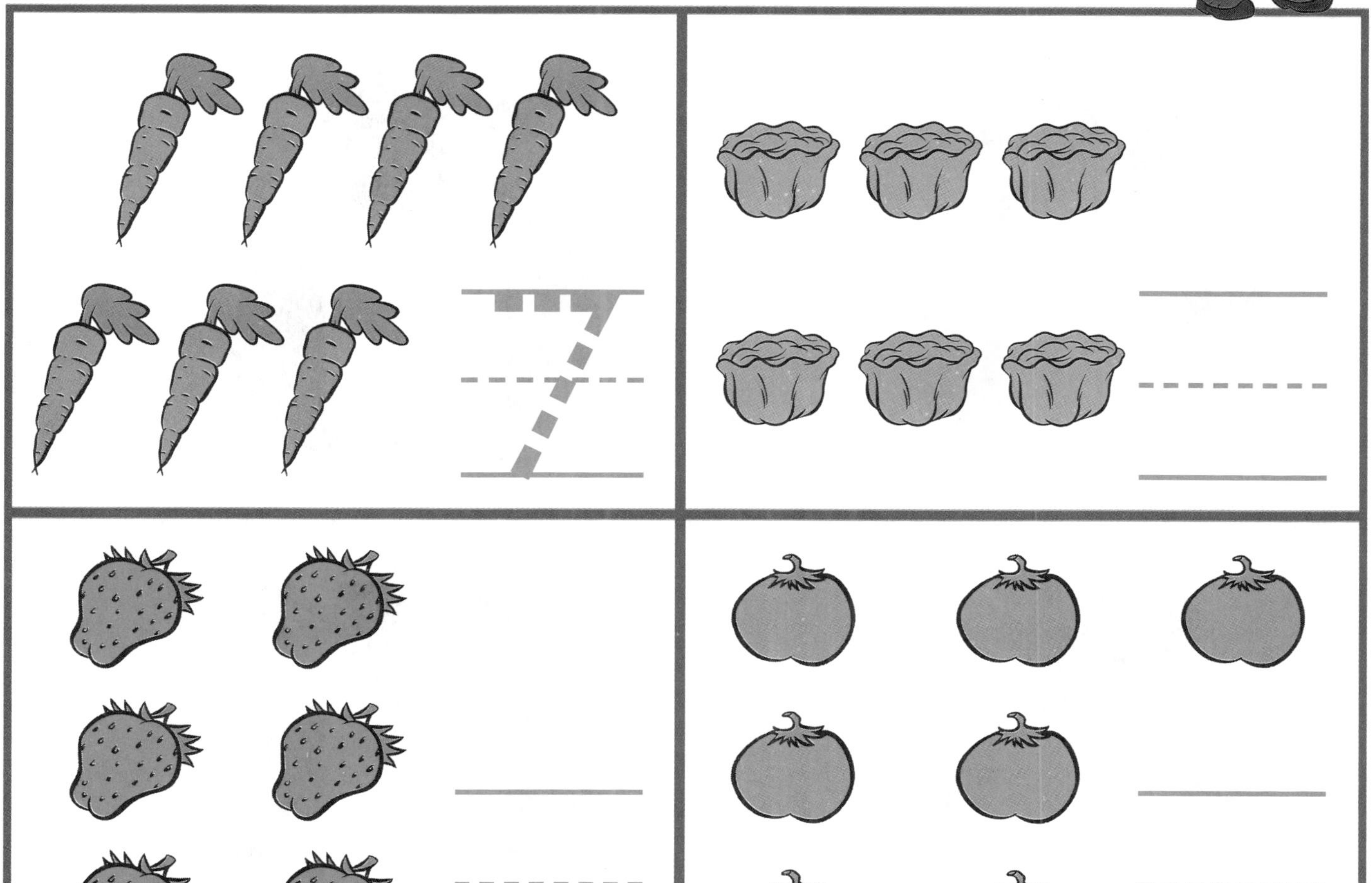

Directions: Have your child count the vegetables in each block, then write 6 or 7 to tell how many.
Skill: Identifying and writing 6 and 7.

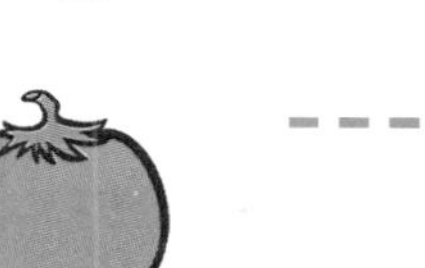

NAME ______________________

EIGHT

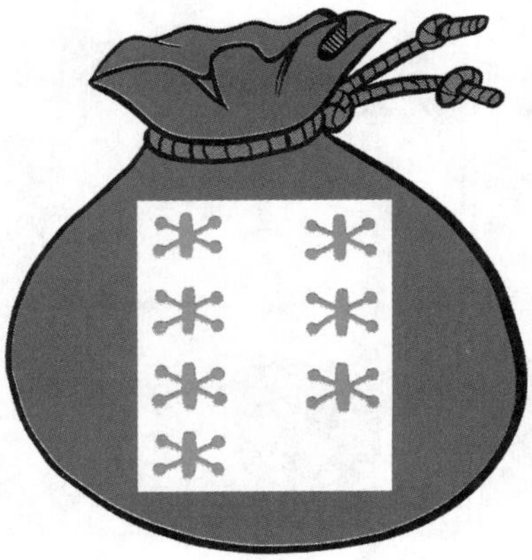

7	8
8	6
5	8

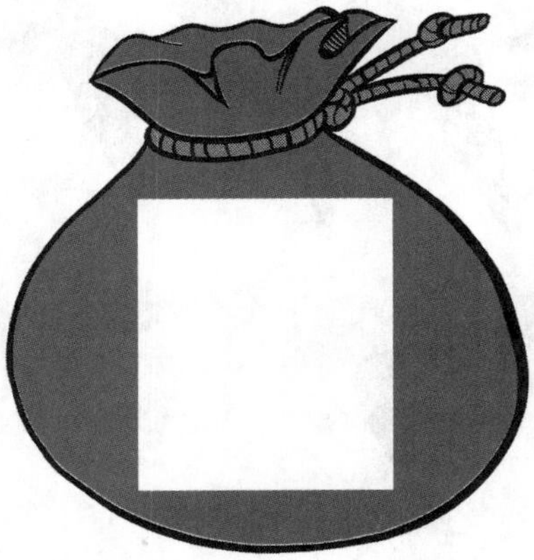

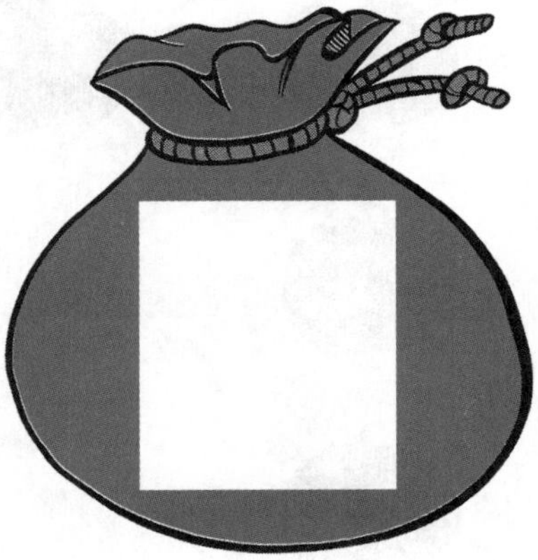

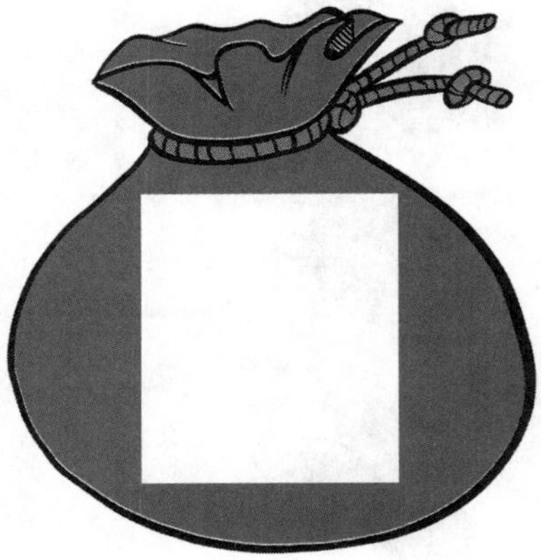

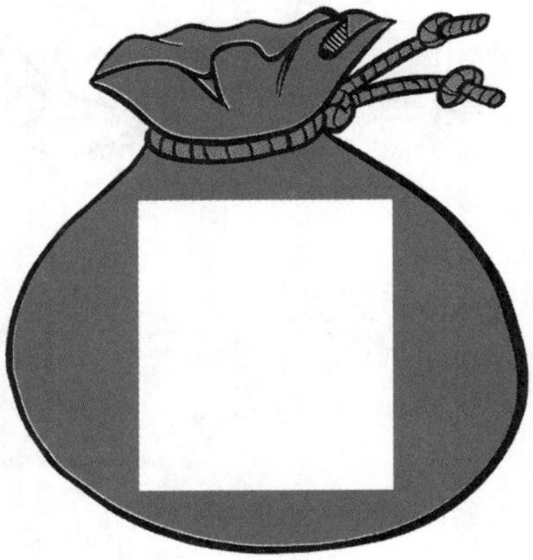

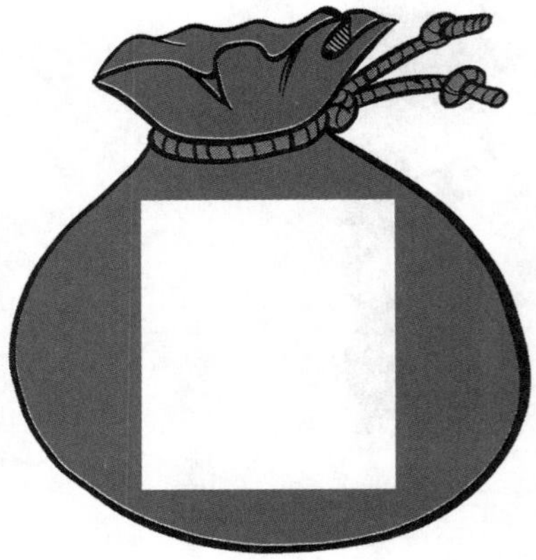

Directions: Have your child draw the correct number of jacks in each bag. ***Skill:*** Identifying groups of five to eight.

NINE

7 8 9

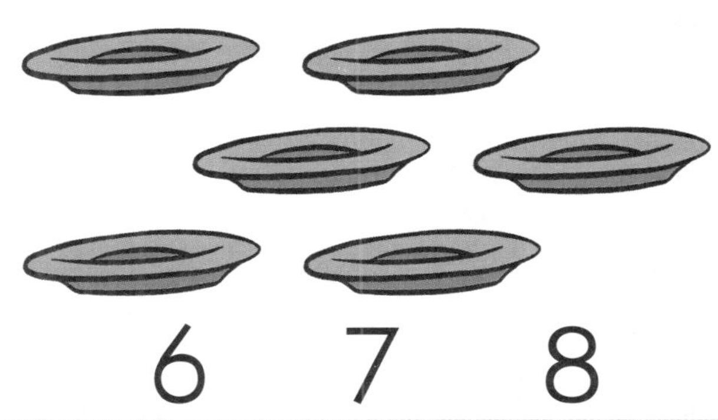

6 7 8

7 8 9

7 8 9

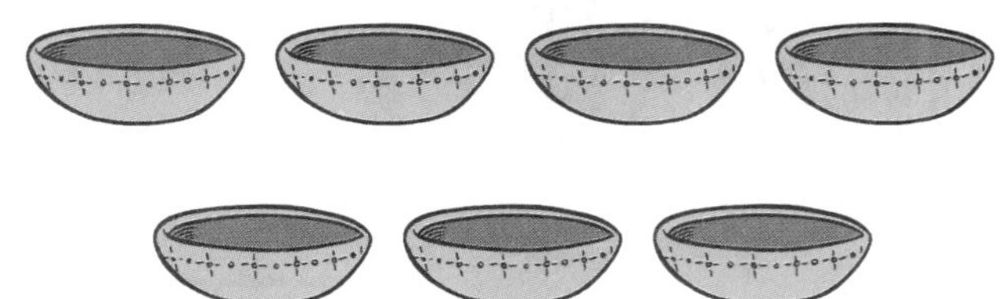

5 6 7

7 8 9

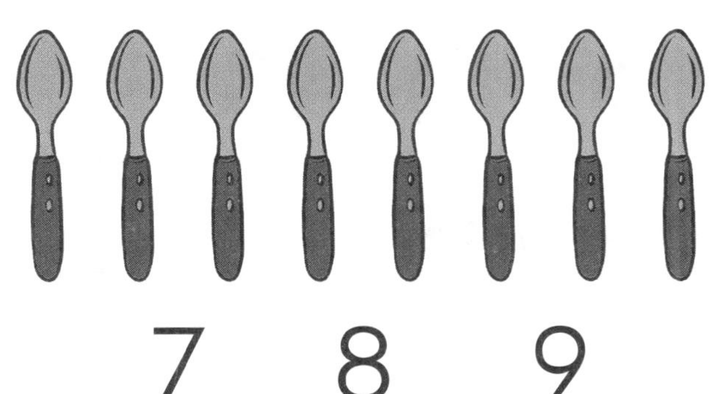

7 8 9

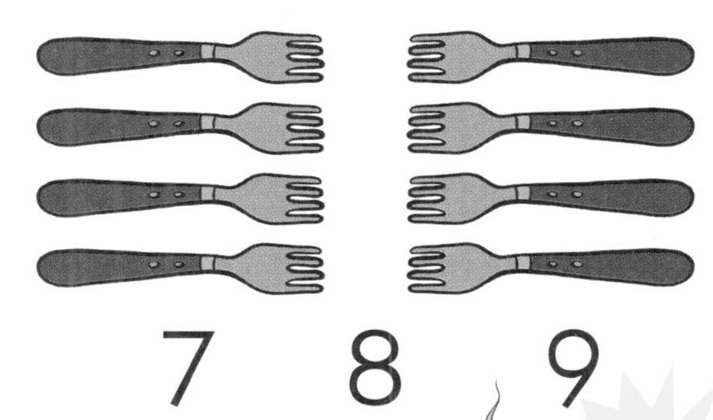

7 8 9

Directions: Have your child count the objects in each block, then circle the correct number to show how many. ***Skill:*** Identifying groups of five to nine.

NAME ____________________

WRITING 8 AND 9

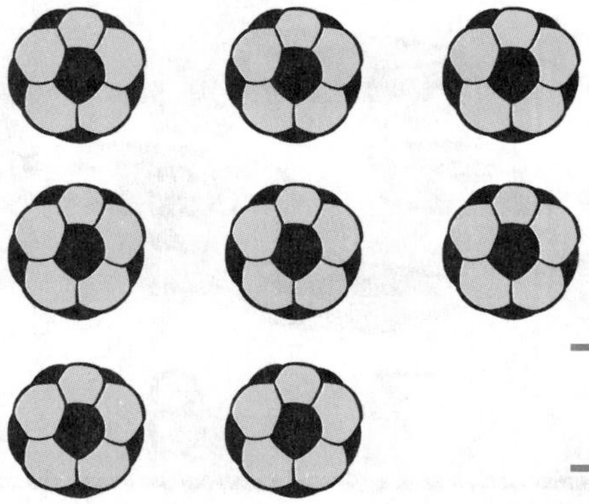

8

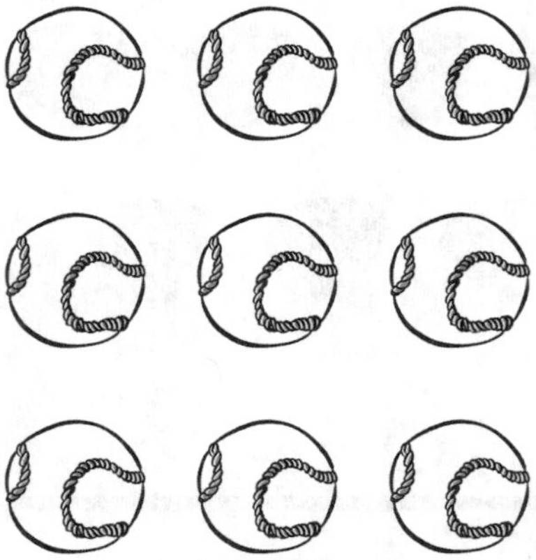

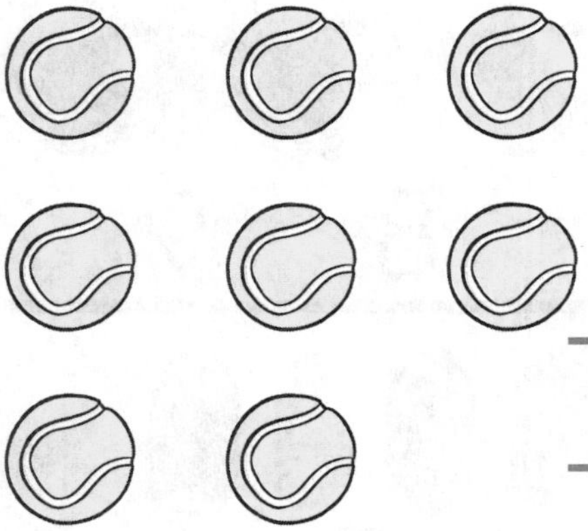

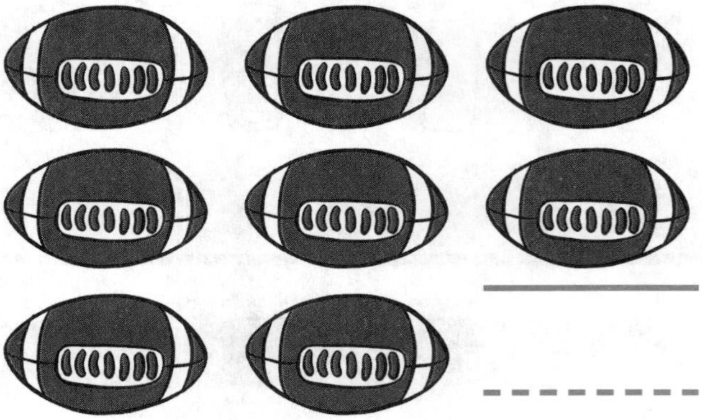

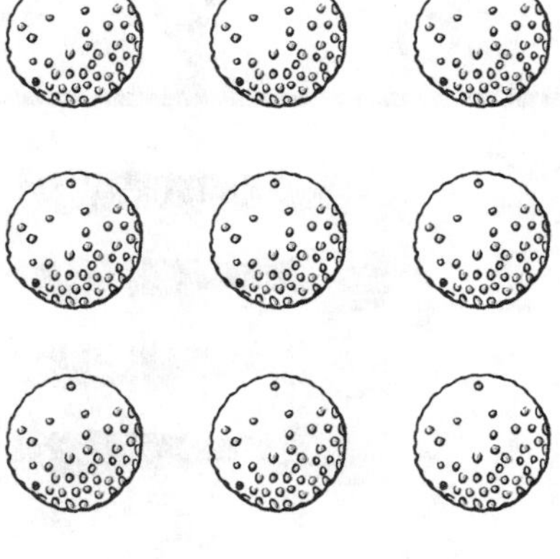

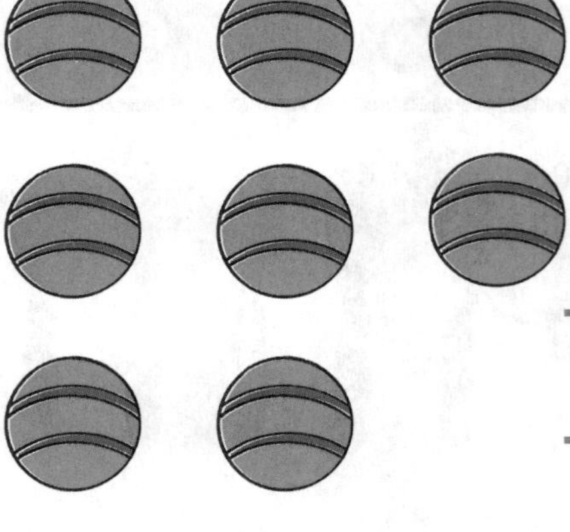

Directions: Have your child count the balls in each block, then write 8 or 9 to tell how many. ***Skill:*** Identifying and writing 8 and 9.

WRITING 10

10 10

10

Directions: Have your child trace, then write the number 10 in the space provided at the top of the page. Ask your child to count the objects in each block, write the number to tell how many, then circle the groups that show 10. ***Skill:*** Identifying and writing 10.

NAME

ORDER 0 TO 10

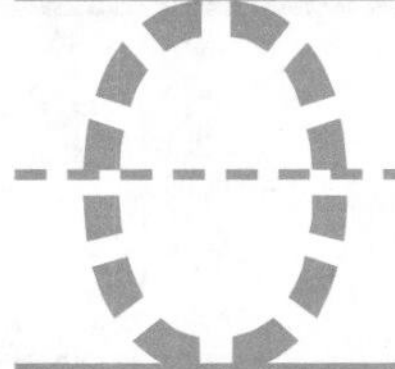

Directions: Have your child count the holes in each poster, then write the numbers in the space provided. ***Skill:*** Identifying number order and writing 0 to 10.

WRITING 11 AND 12

Directions: Have your child trace, then write the numbers 11 and 12 in the space provided at the top of the page. Ask your child to count the pieces of fruit in each block, then write 11 or 12 to tell how many. ***Skill:*** Identifying and writing 11 and 12.

NAME ______________________________

TIME—HOUR

4 o'clock

4:00

1 o'clock

1:00

___ o'clock

___:00

___ o'clock

___:00

___ o'clock

___:______

___ o'clock

___:______

___ o'clock

___:______

___ o'clock

___:______

___ o'clock

___:______

___ o'clock

___:______

Directions: Explain to your child that the two clocks at the top of the page show the same time. Following the example, have your child write the time for each clock.
Skill: Identifying time by the hour.

TIME—HOUR

Show this time on this clock.	Show this time on this clock.
 9:00 	  10:00
 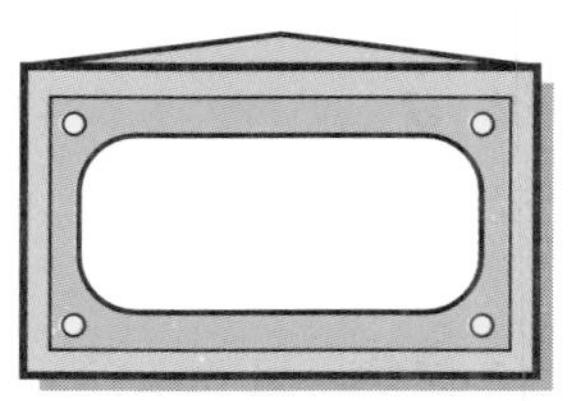	 11:00 
 5:00 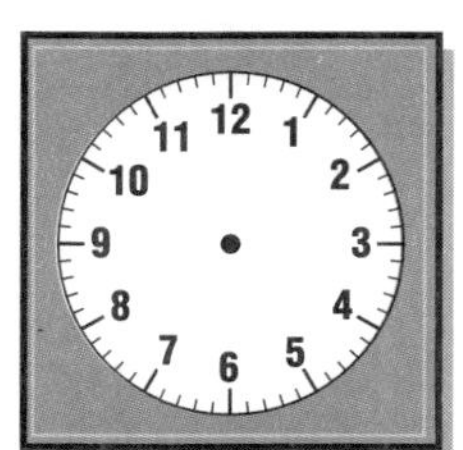	 6:00 
 	 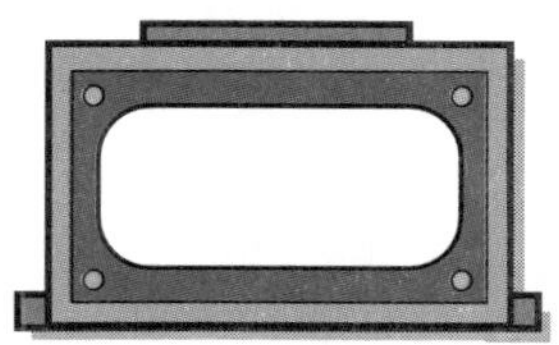

Directions: Following the example at the top of the page, have your child write the time for each clock.
Skill: Identifying time by the hour.

NAME ______________________________

TIME—HALF HOUR

 1 o'clock 1:00	 one thirty 1:30	 2 o'clock 2:00
 two thirty 2 : 30	 _____ thirty ___: 30	 ____ thirty ___: 30
 _______ thirty ___:______	 _______ thirty ___:______	 ____ thirty ___:______
 __ thirty ___:______	 ___ thirty ___:______	 _____ thirty ___:______

Directions: Explain to your child the time that is shown on each clock at the top of the page. Following the example, have your child write the time for each clock. ***Skill:*** Identifying time by the half-hour.

Show this time on this clock.

11:30

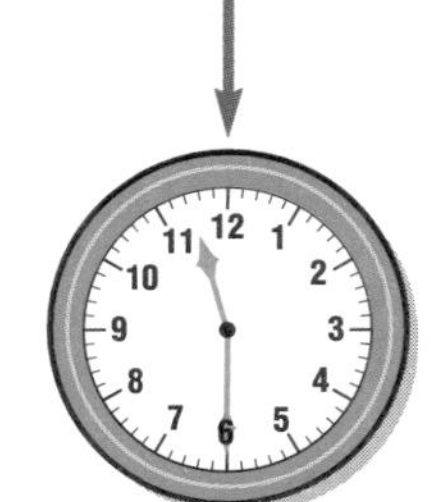

Show this time on this clock.

Directions: Following the example at the top of the page, have your child write the time for each clock.
Skill: Identifying time by the half-hour.

NAME ______________________________

PENNY AND NICKEL

1 penny
1¢

5 pennies
5¢

1 nickel
5¢

5 ¢

_____¢

_____¢

_____¢

_____¢

_____¢

_____¢

_____¢

Directions: Show your child the coins at the top of the page and explain the value of each. Then have your child count the coins in each block and write the amount.
Skill: Identifying and counting pennies and nickels.

PENNY, NICKEL AND DIME

1 penny
1¢

1 nickel
5¢

1 dime
10¢

_____¢

_____¢

_____¢

_____¢

_____¢

_____¢

_____¢

_____¢

Directions: Have your child look at the coins at the top of the page and explain the value of each. Then have your child count the coins in each block and write the amount. ***Skill:*** Identifying and counting pennies, nickels and dimes.

NAME ______________________________

PROBLEM SOLVING

 10 pennies = 10¢		I dime = 10¢
I have	**I buy**	**I have left**
	 5¢	9¢ - 5¢ ___ ¢
	 6¢	¢ - ¢ ___ ¢
	 8¢	¢ - ¢ ___ ¢
	 5¢	¢ - ¢ ___ ¢

Directions: Show your child the coins at the top of the page and explain the value of each. Then, following the example, have your child calculate the amount of money left.
Skill: Counting money.

NAME ______________________________

Inch

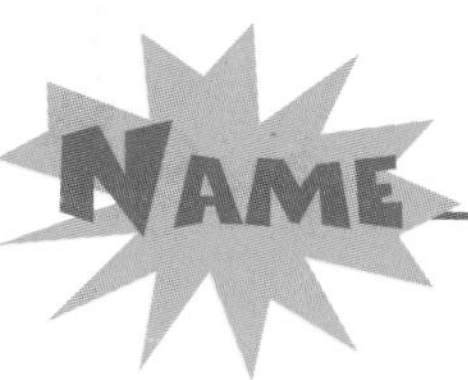

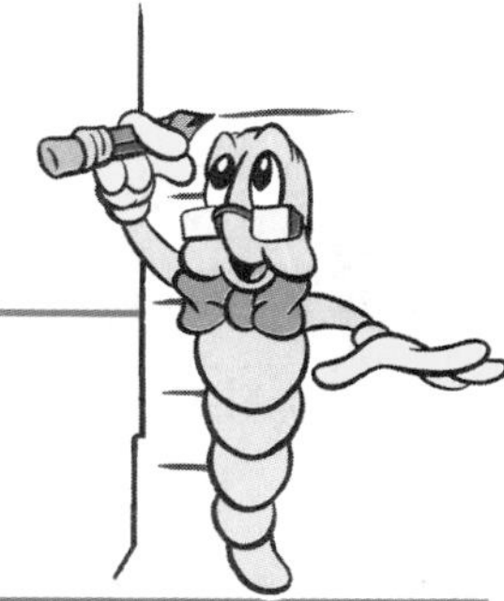

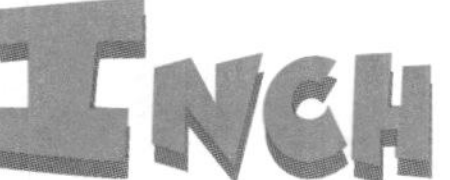

1 inch

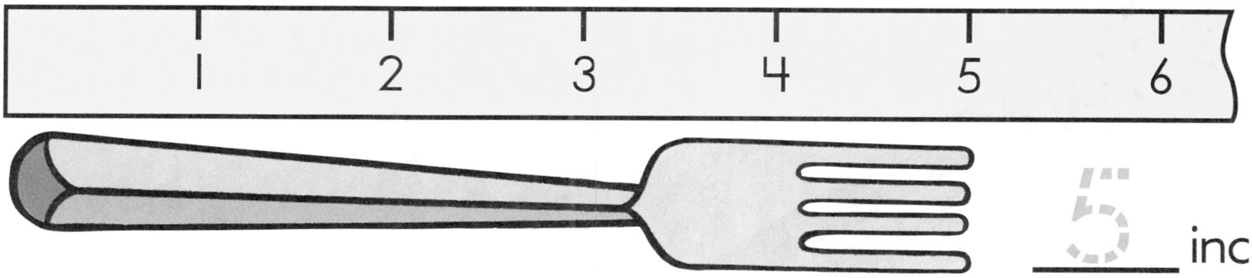
1
2
3
4
5
6

5 inches

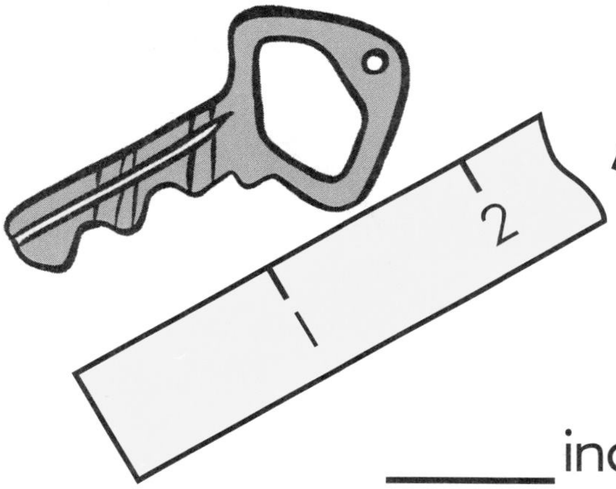
1
2

_____ inches

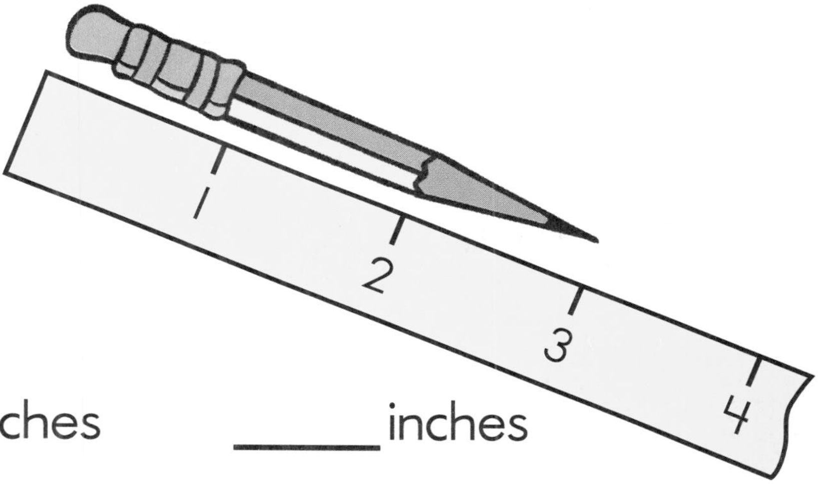
1
2
3
4

_____ inches

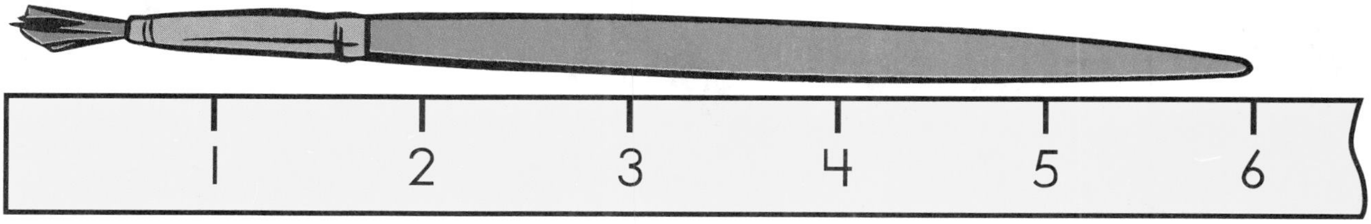
1
2
3
4
5
6

_____ inches

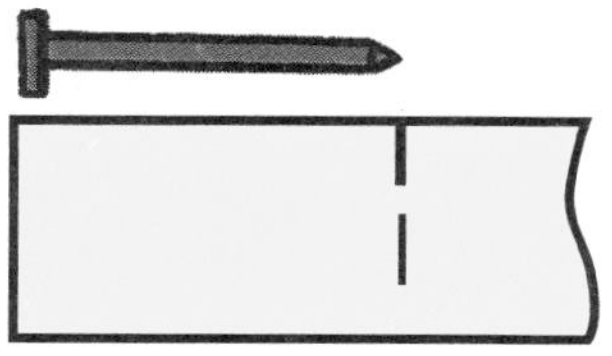
1

_____ inch

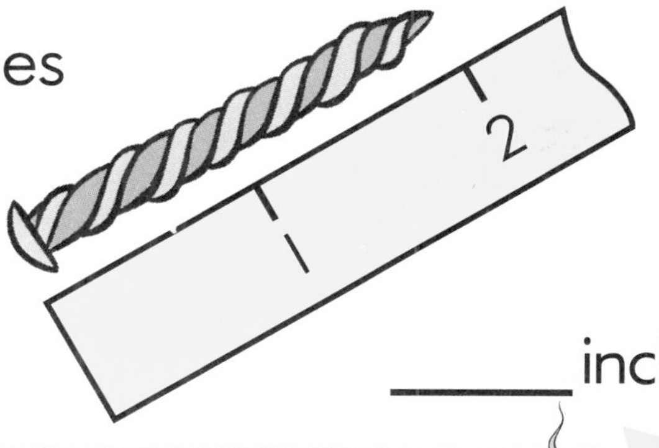
1
2

_____ inches

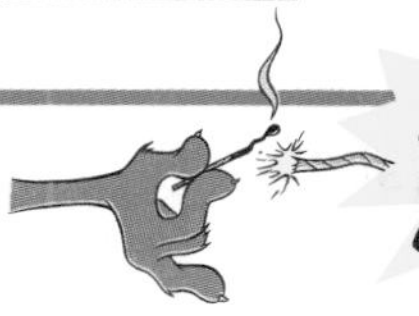

Directions: Following the example at the top of the page, have your child measure and write the number of inches in the space provided below each object. ***Skill:*** Measuring length in inches.

NAME ________________________________

INCH

_____inches

_____inches

_____inches

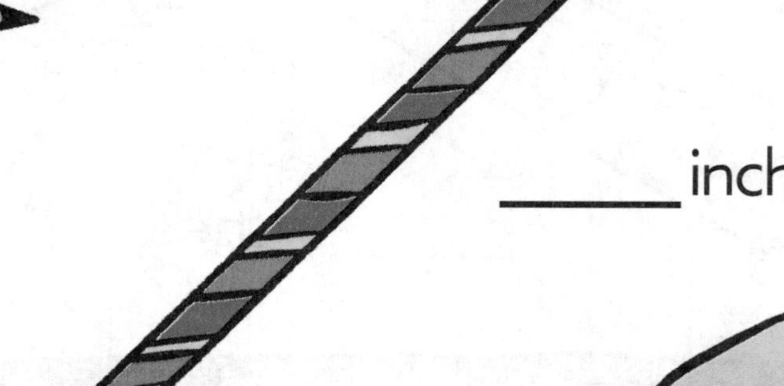

_____inches

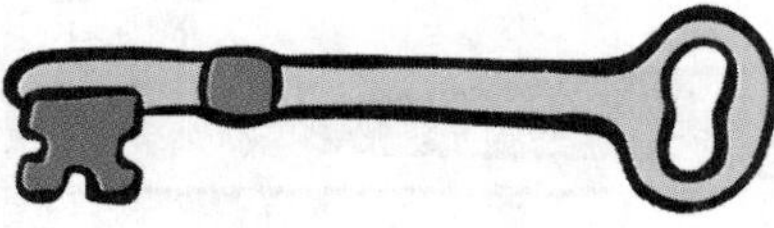

_____inches

_____inch

_____inches

Directions: Using your own ruler, have your child measure and write the number of inches in the space provided below each object. ***Skill:*** Measuring length in inches.

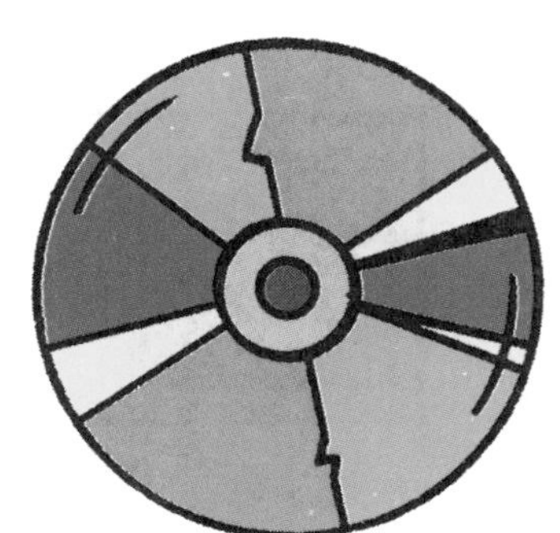

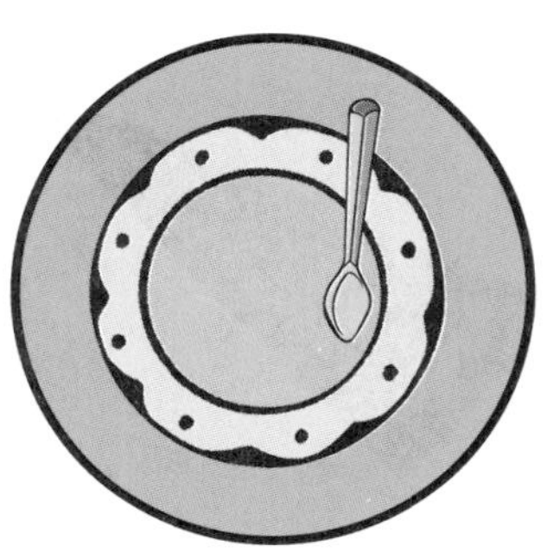

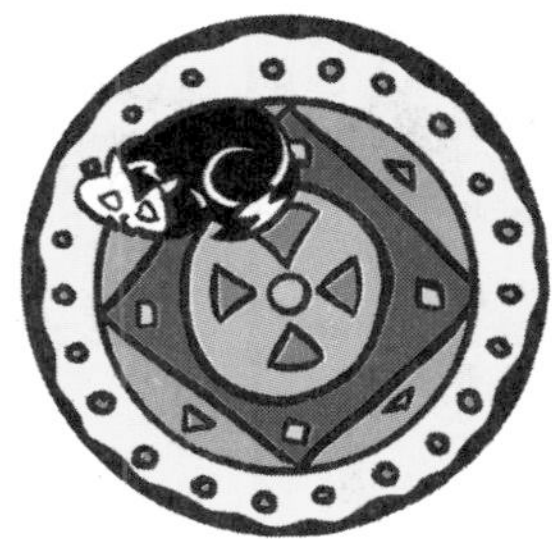

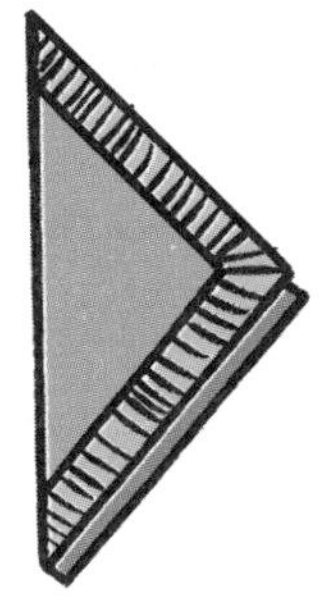

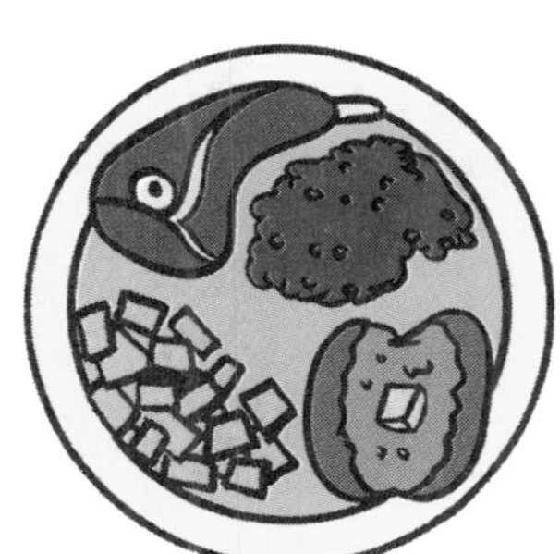

Directions: Have your child look at the pictures, then place an X on each object that has the shape of a circle. ***Skill:*** Identifying a circle.

NAME ______________________________

SQUARE

Directions: Have your child look at the pictures, then circle each object that has the shape of a square. ***Skill:*** Identifying a square.

NAME ______________________________

TRIANGLE

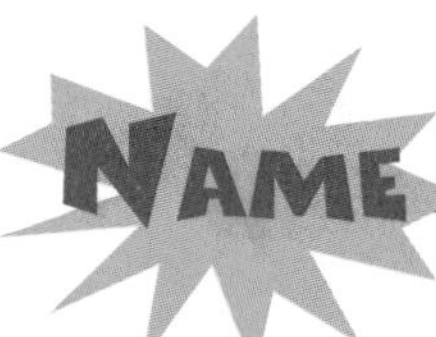

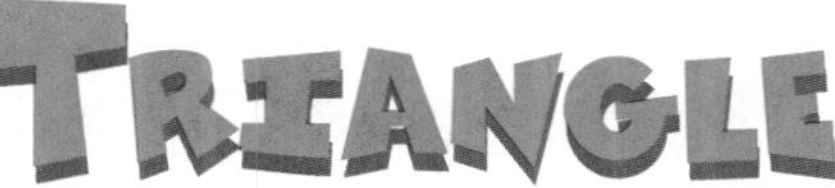

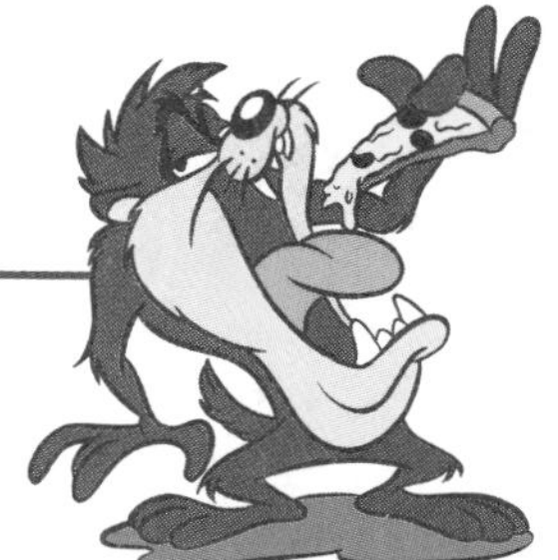

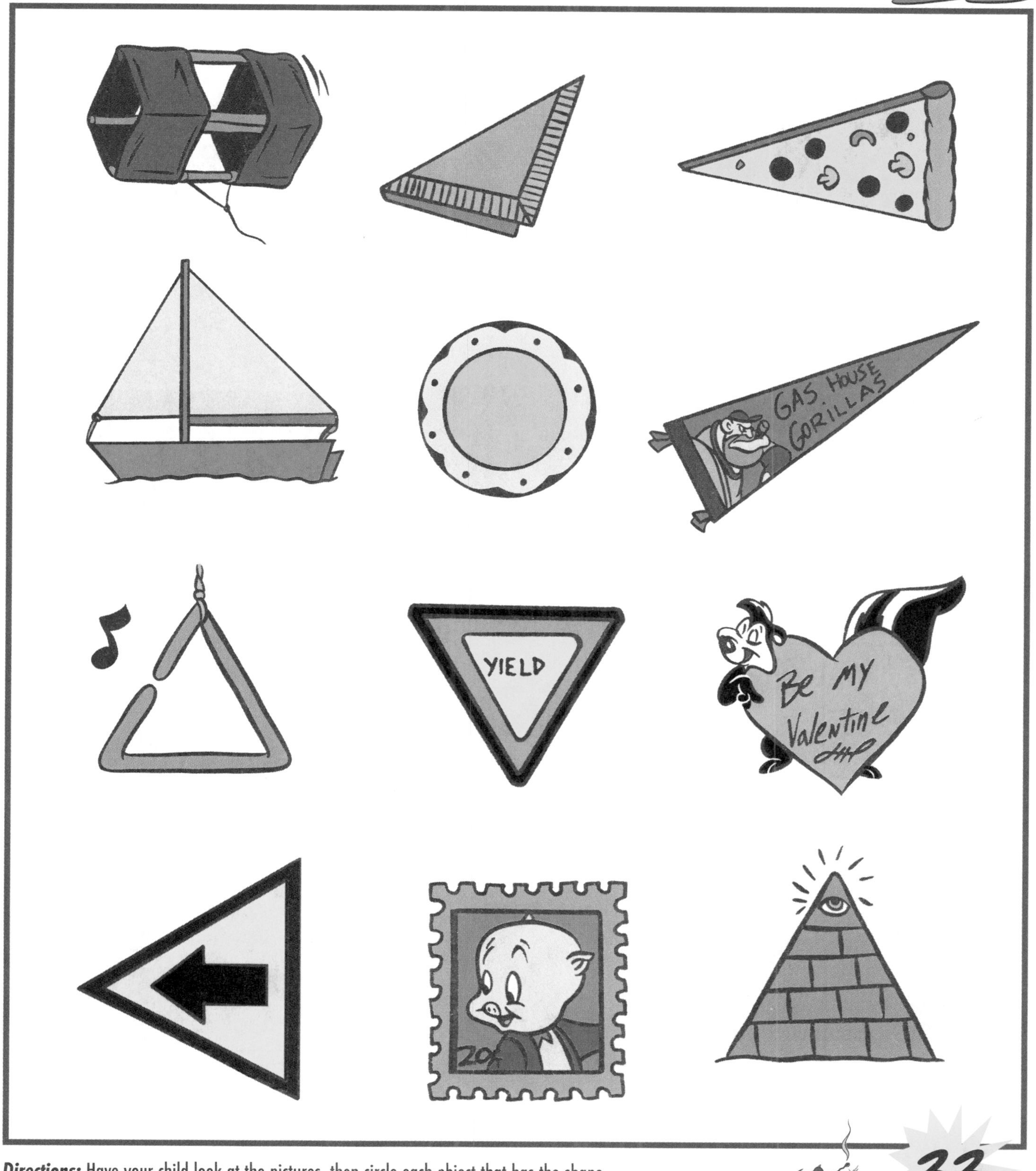

Directions: Have your child look at the pictures, then circle each object that has the shape of a triangle. ***Skill:*** Identifying a triangle.

NAME ______________________________

RECTANGLE

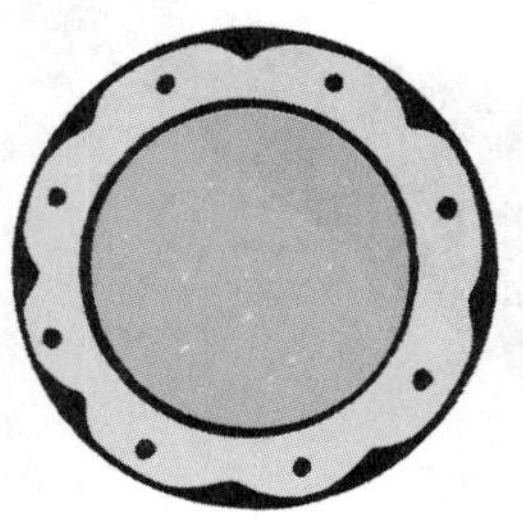

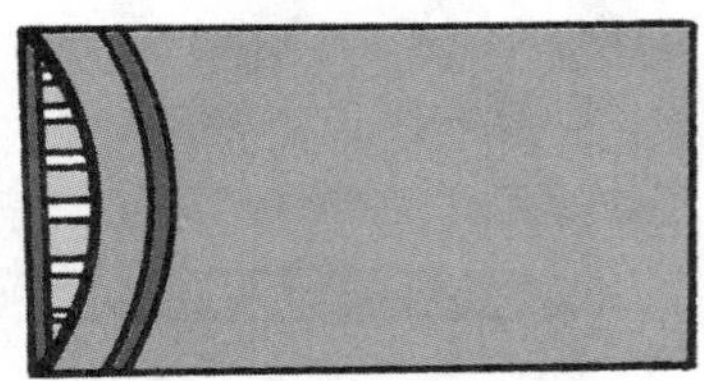

Directions: Have your child look at the pictures, then circle each object that has the shape of a rectangle. ***Skill:*** Identifying a rectangle.

COUNTING AND MATCHING

Directions: Have your child count the objects in each block on the left, then draw a line to the block on the right that has the same number of objects. ***Skill:*** Counting and matching objects.

NAME

COUNTING AND MATCHING

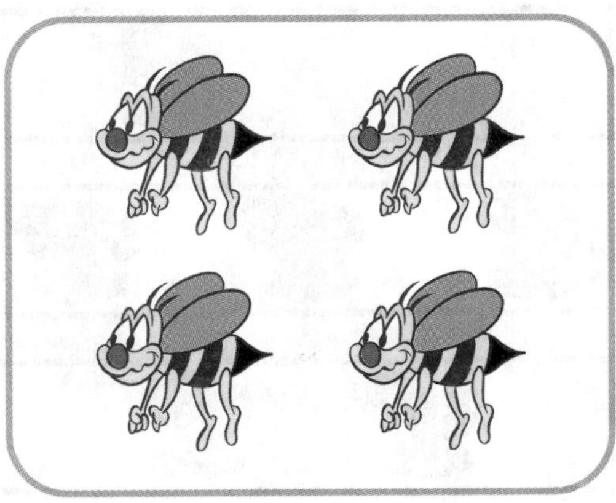

Directions: Have your child count the objects in each block on the left, then draw a line to the block on the right that has the same number of objects. ***Skill:*** Counting and matching objects.

Counting and Matching

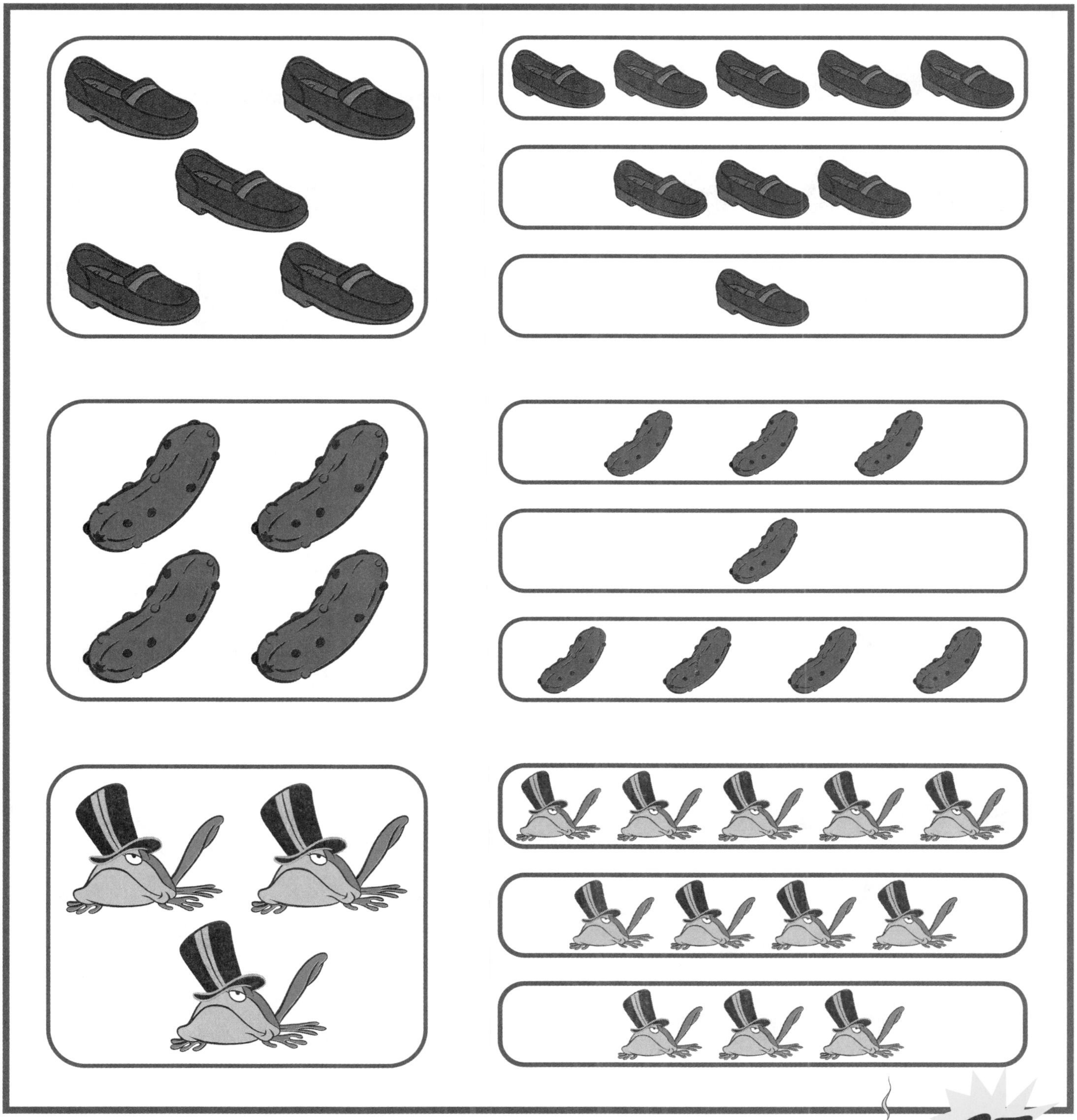

Directions: Have your child count the objects in each block on the left, then draw a line to the block on the right that has the same number of objects. ***Skill:*** Counting and matching objects.

NAME

Counting and Matching

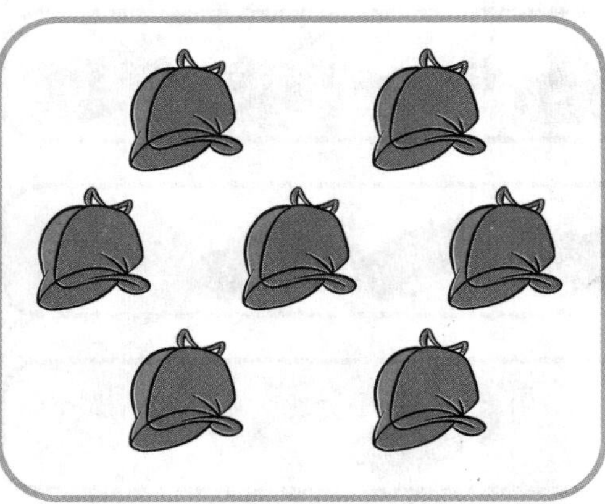

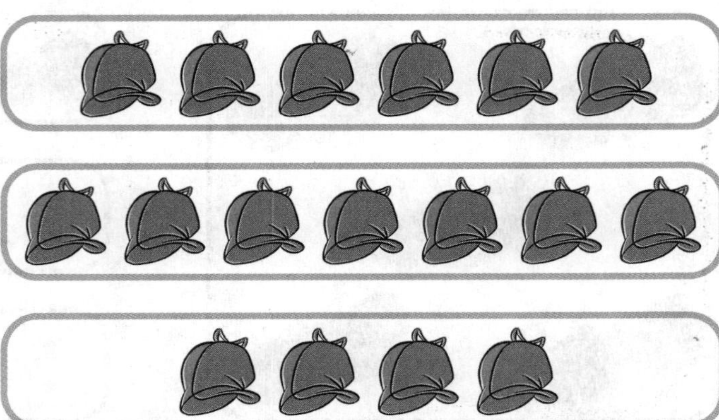

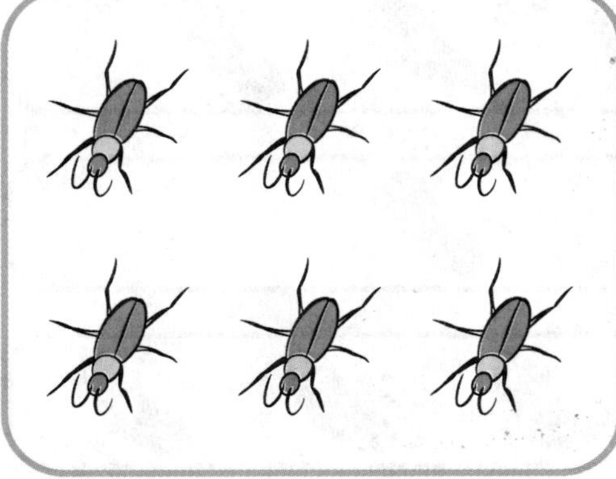

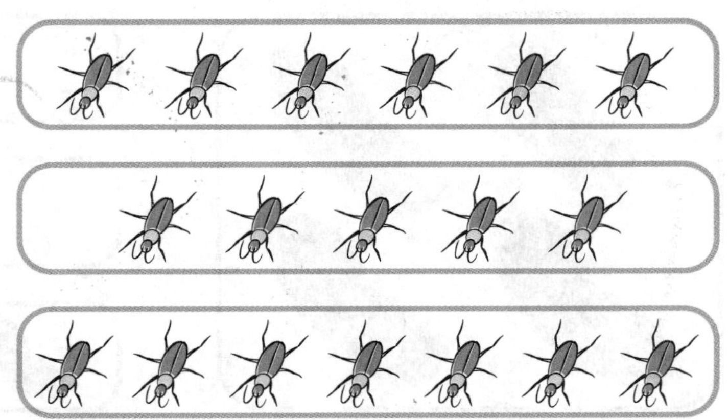

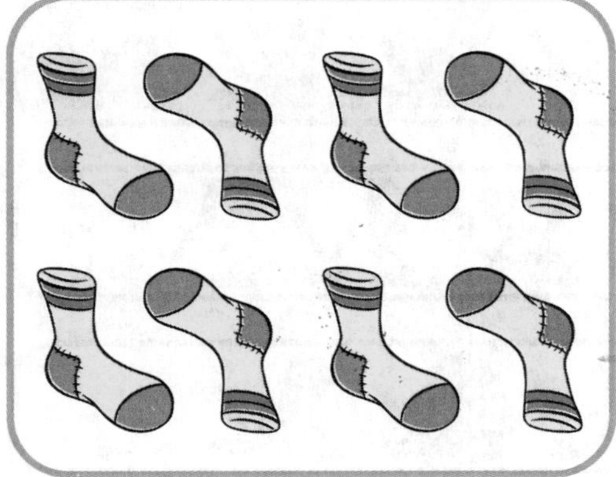

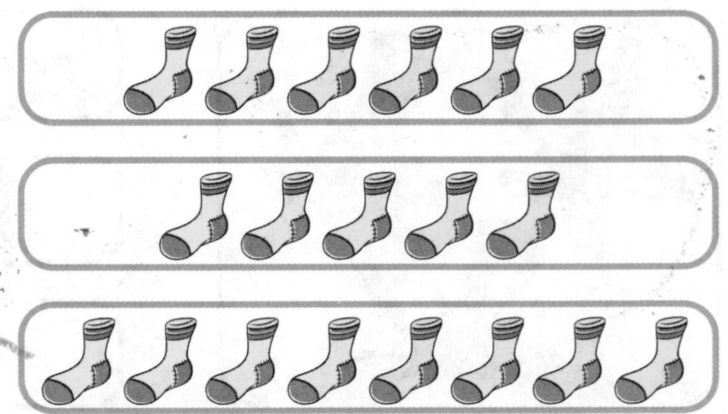

Directions: Have your child count the objects in each block on the left, then draw a line to the block on the right that has the same number of objects. ***Skill:*** Counting and matching objects.

Counting and Matching

QUANTUM LEAP THEORY

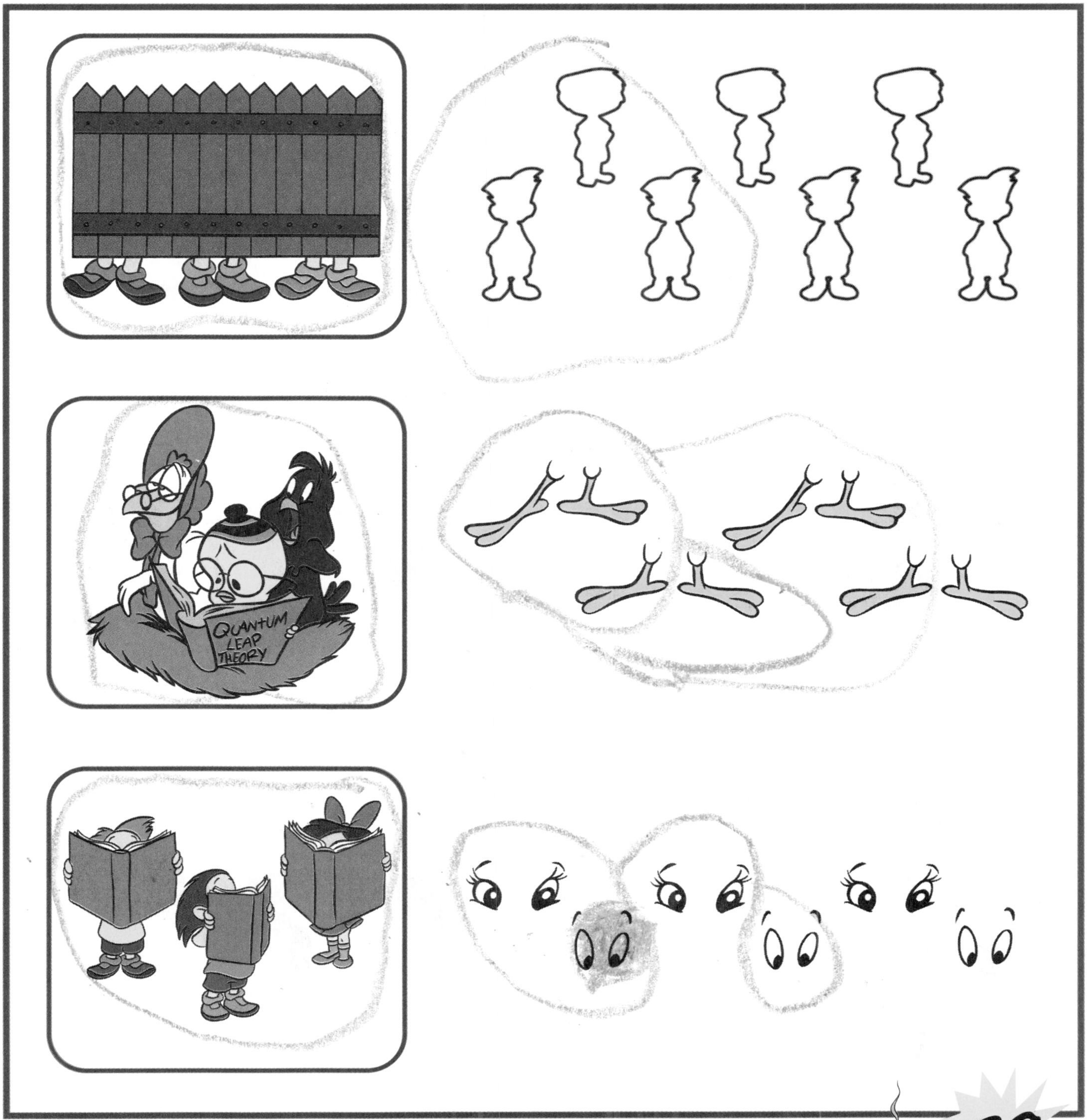

Directions: Have your child count the objects on the left, then circle the same number of items that correspond to those objects on the right. **_Skill:_** Counting and matching by inference.

NAME ______________________

COUNTING AND MATCHING

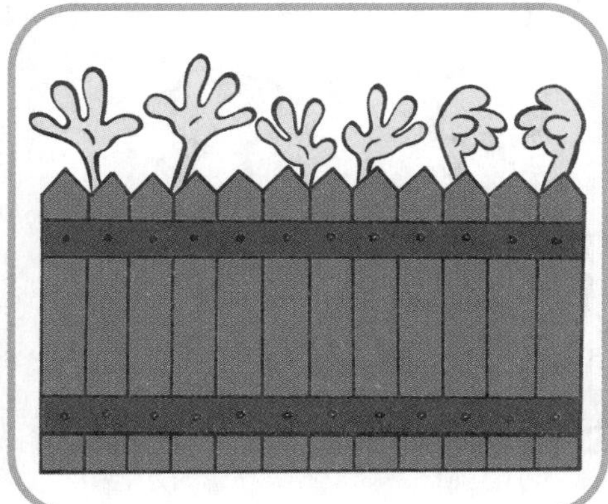

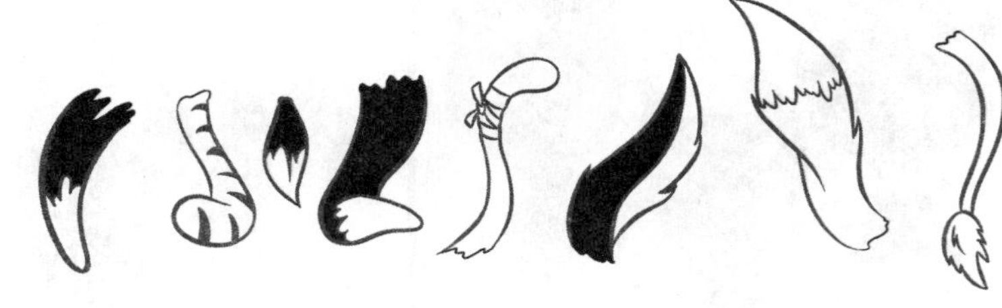

Directions: Have your child count the objects on the left, then circle the same number of items that correspond to those objects on the right. ***Skill:*** Counting and matching by inference.

COUNTING AND MATCHING

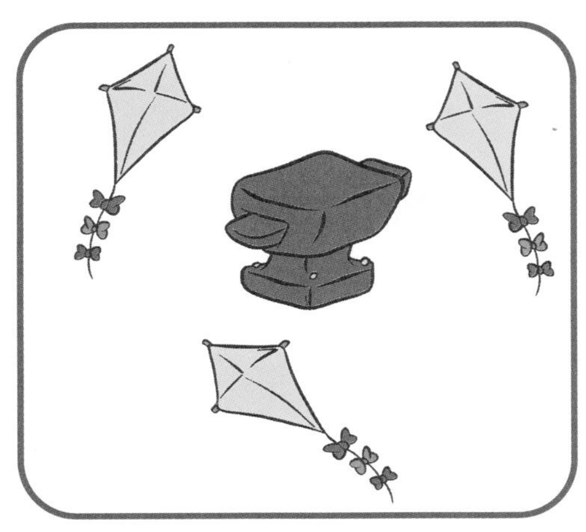

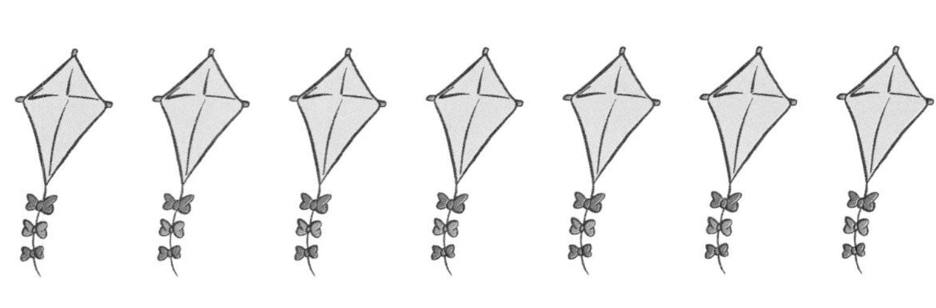

Directions: Have your child identify the objects on the right, then count the number of those objects in the box on the left. Your child should then circle the same number of objects on the right.
Skill: Counting and matching objects.

NAME

Counting and Matching

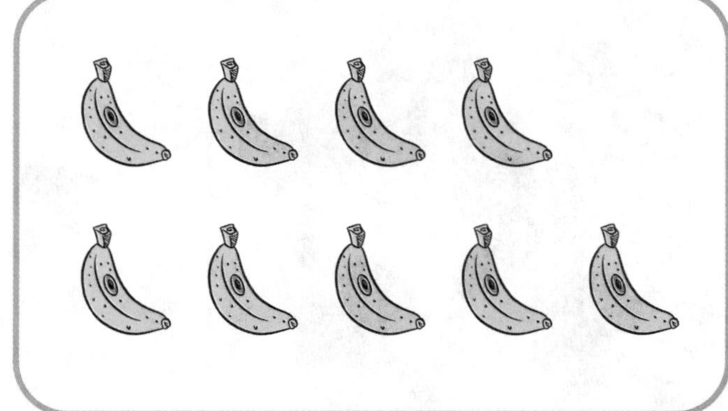

Directions: **Have your child count the objects in each box on the left and then circle the same number of objects in the box on the right. *Skill:* Counting and matching objects.**

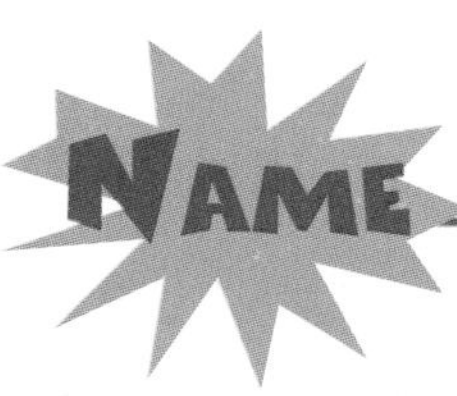

COUNTING AND MATCHING

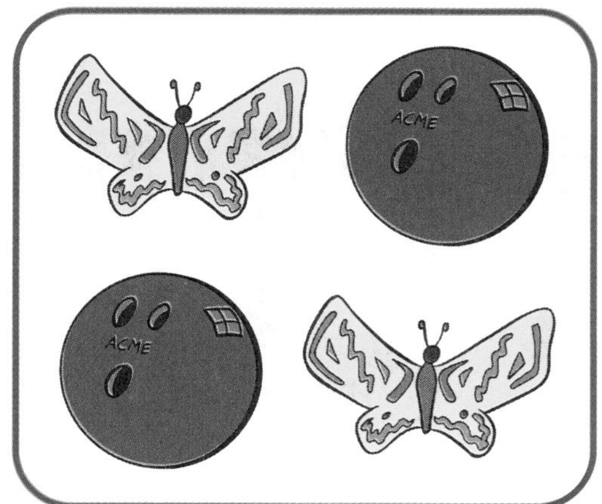

Directions: Have your child identify the objects in each box on the right, then count the number of those same objects in the box on the left. Ask your child to circle the same number of objects in the box on the right. ***Skill:*** Counting and matching objects.

NAME ______________________________

COUNTING AND MATCHING

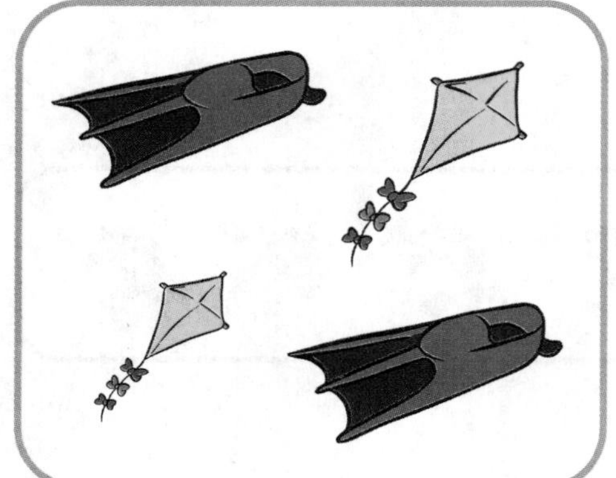

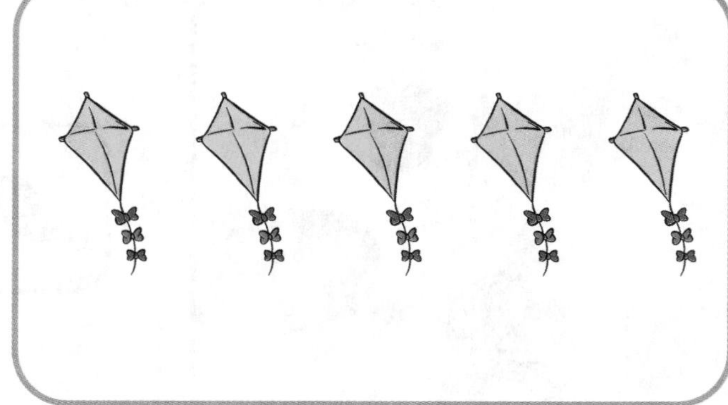

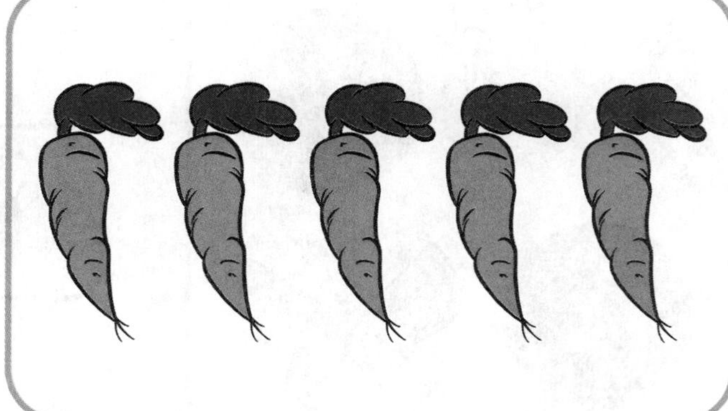

Directions: Have your child identify the objects in the each box on the right, then count the number of those same objects in the box on the left. Ask your child to circle the same number of objects in the box on the right. ***Skill:*** Counting and matching objects.

ONE MORE

Directions: Have your child draw a line from each large box on the left to the small box at the right that contains one more. ***Skill:*** Identifying one more.

NAME ________________

ONE MORE

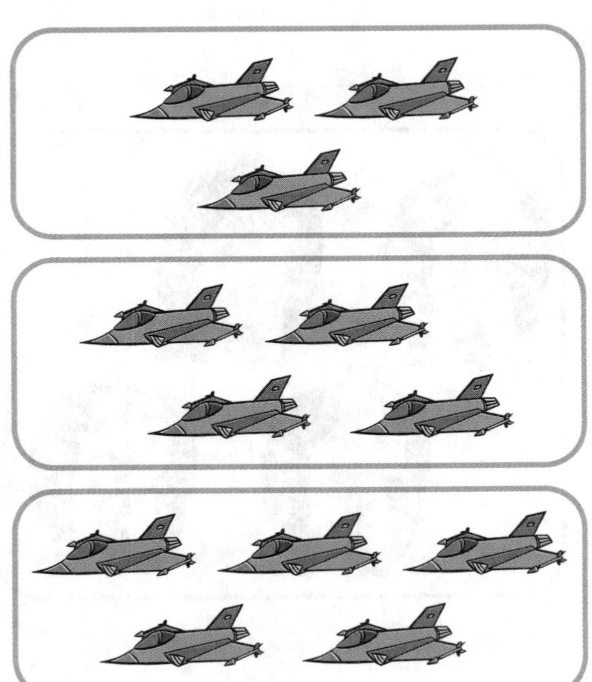

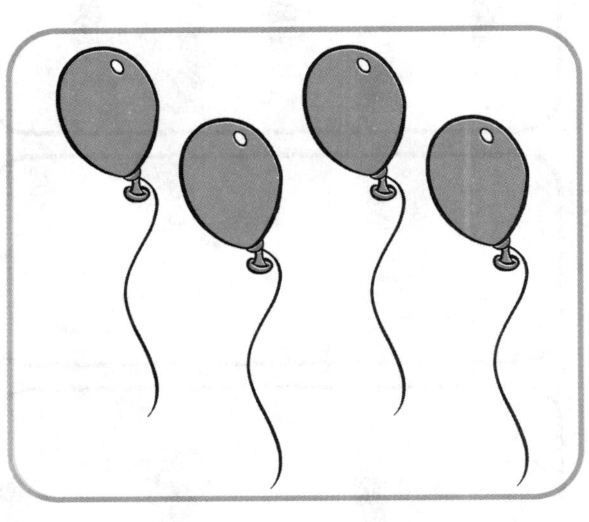

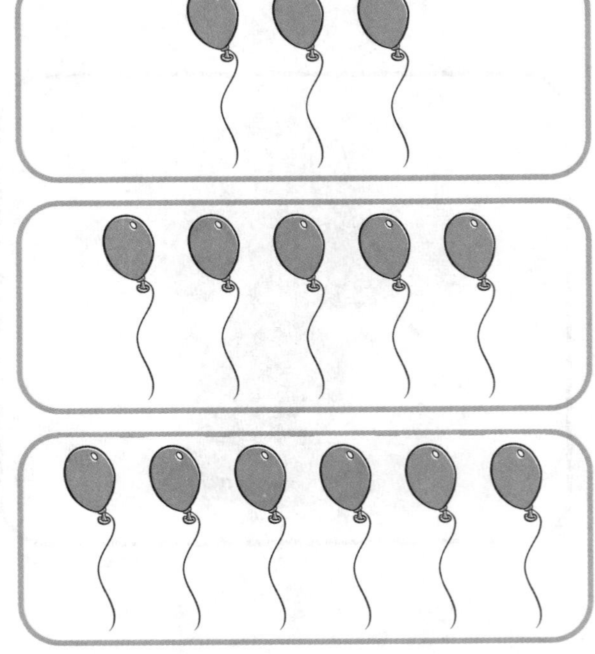

Directions: Have your child draw a line from each large box on the left to the small box at the right that contains one more. ***Skill:*** Identifying one more.

ONE MORE

Directions: Have your child draw a line from each large box on the left to the small box at the right that contains one more. ***Skill:*** Identifying one more.

NAME

ONE MORE

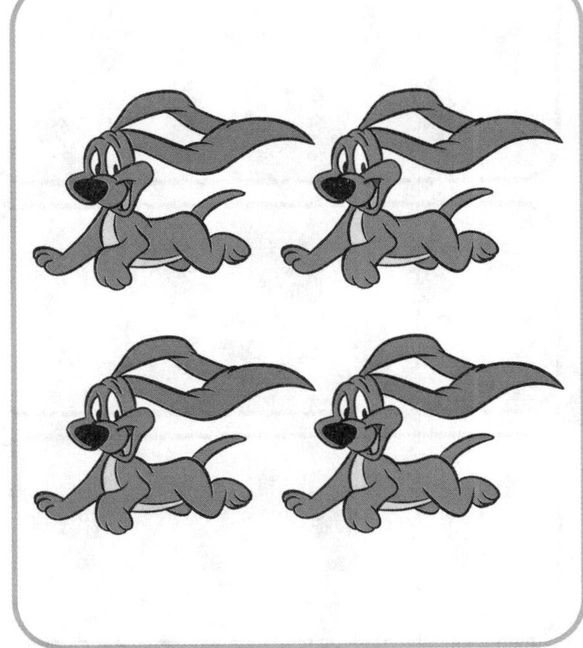

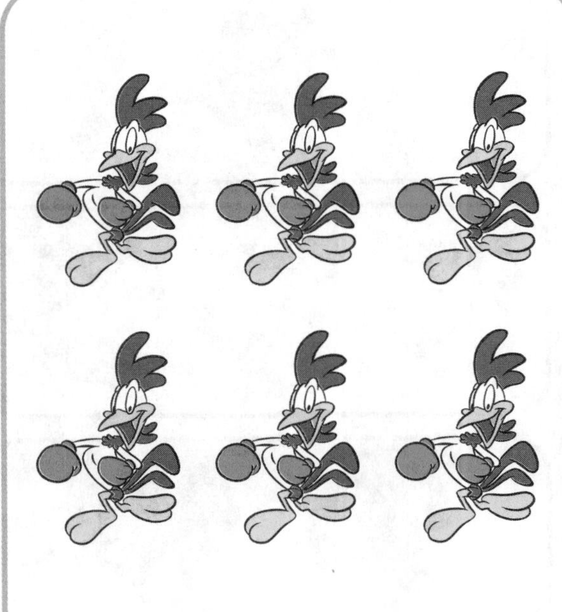

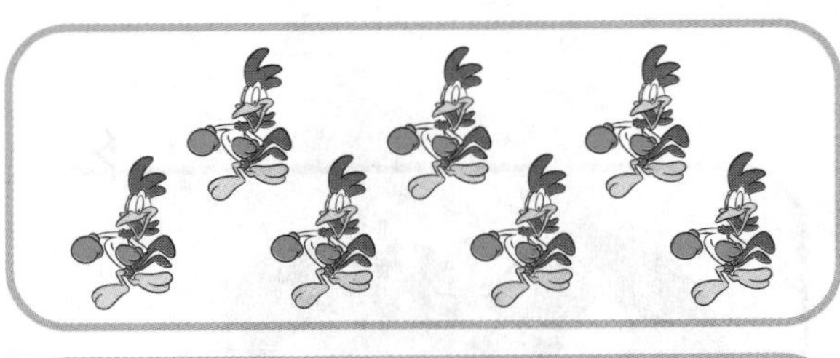

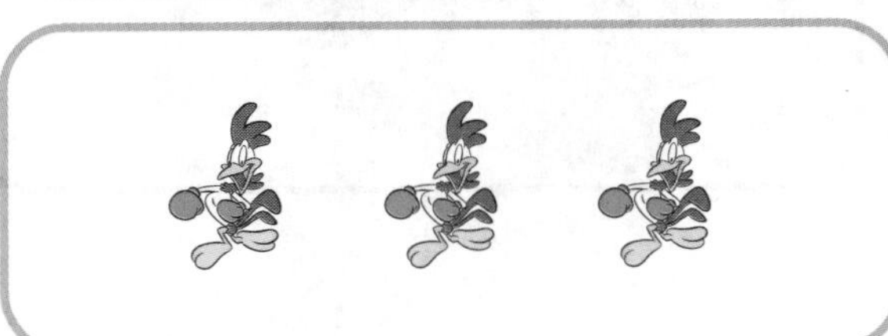

Directions: Have your child draw a line from each large box on the left to the small box at the right that contains one more. ***Skill:*** Identifying one more.

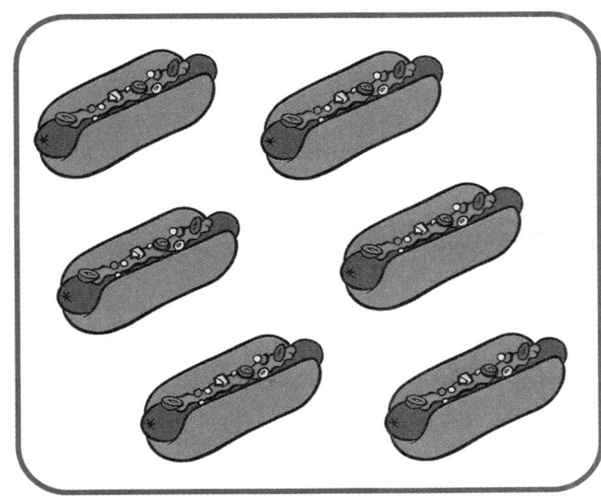

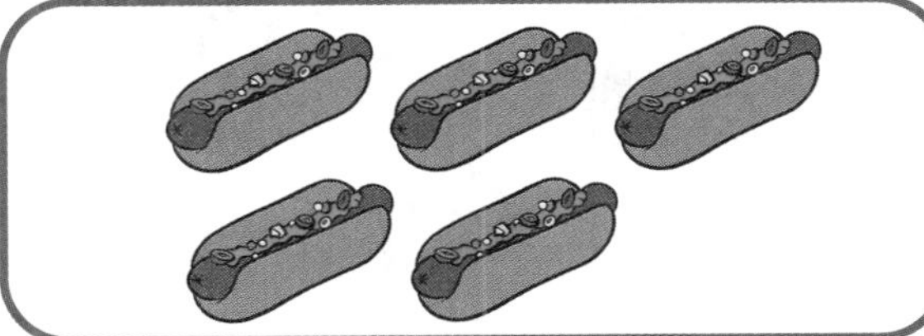

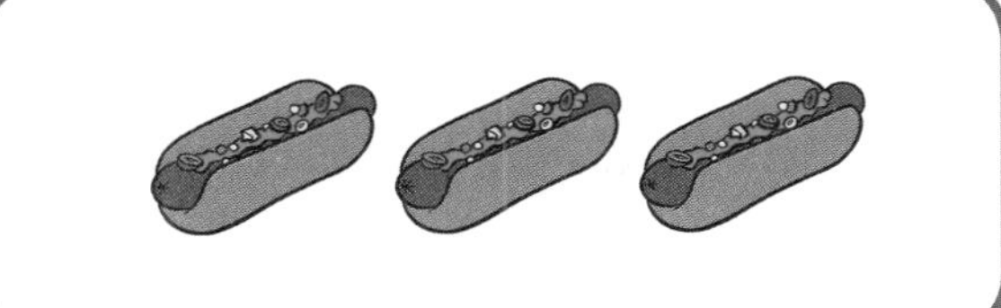

Directions: Have your child draw a line from each large box on the left to the small box at the right that contains one more. ***Skill:*** Identifying one more.

NAME ___

ONE MORE

Directions: Have your child draw a line from each large box on the left to the small box at the right that contains one more. ***Skill:*** Identifying one more.

ONE LESS

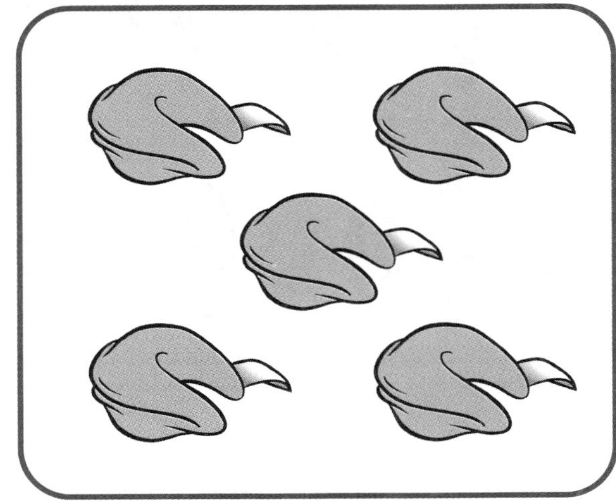

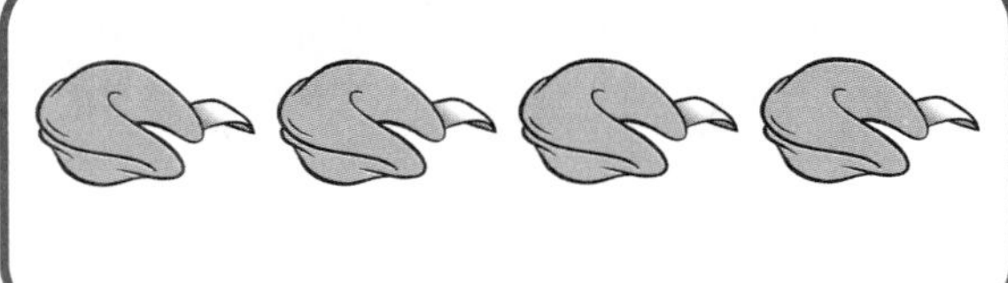

Directions: Have your child draw a line from each large box on the left to the small box at the right that contains one less. ***Skill:*** Identifying one less.

NAME

ONE LESS

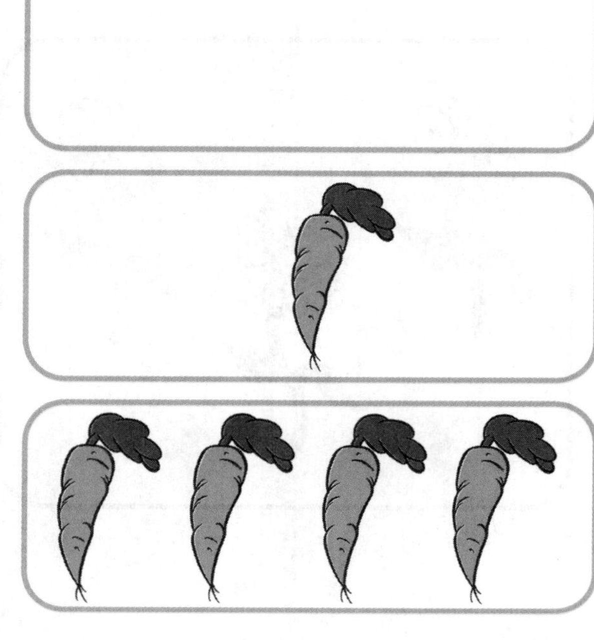

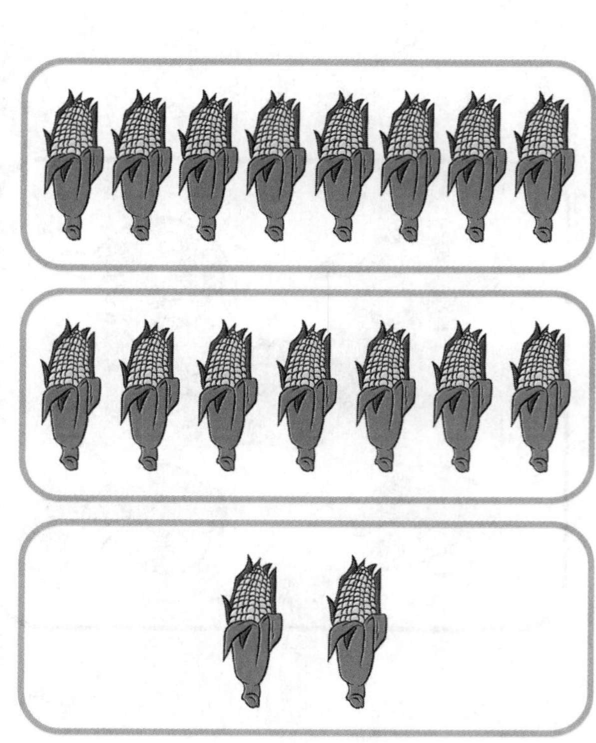

Directions: Have your child draw a line from each large box on the left to the small box at the right that contains one less. ***Skill:*** Identifying one less.

ONE LESS

Directions: Have your child draw a line from each large box on the left to the small box at the right that contains one less. ***Skill:*** Identifying one less.

NAME ____________________

ONE LESS

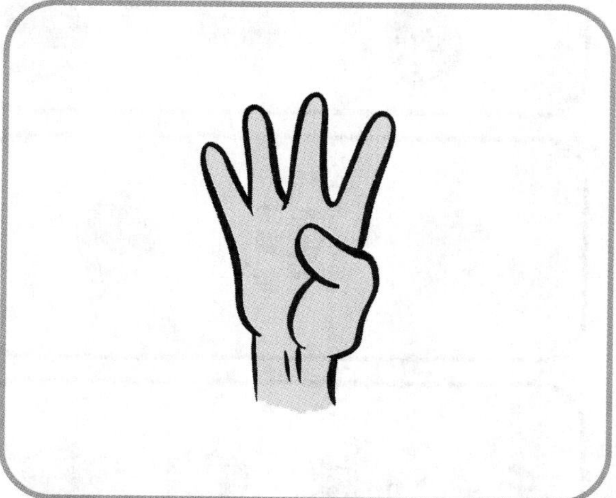

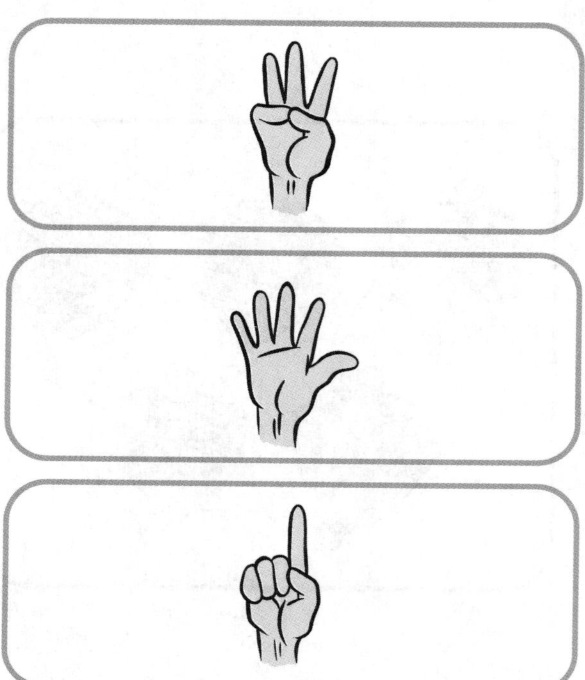

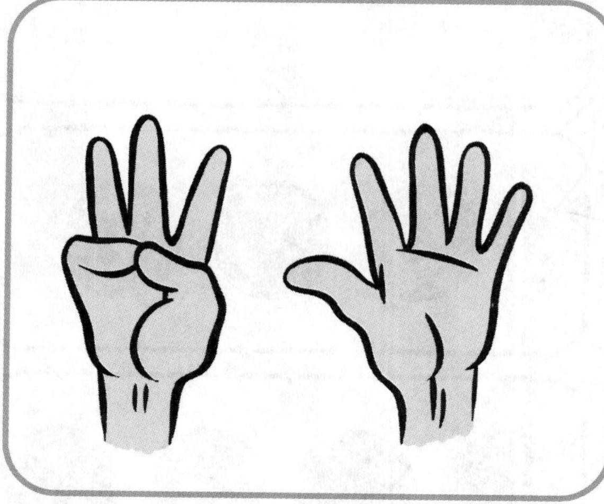

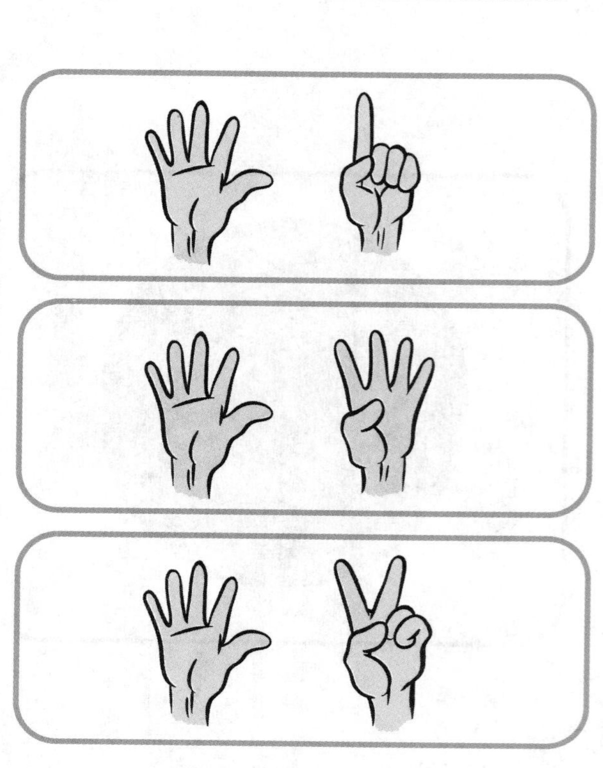

Directions: Have your child draw a line from each large box on the left to the small box at the right that contains one less. ***Skill:*** Identifying one less.

NAME

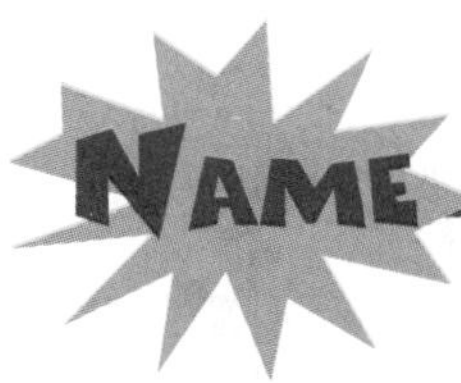

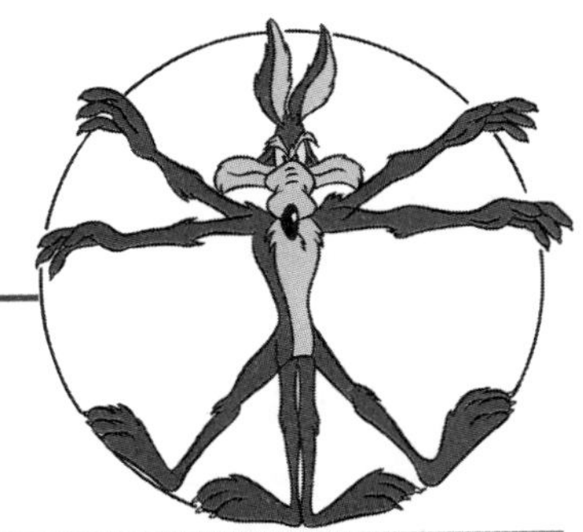

PATTERNS

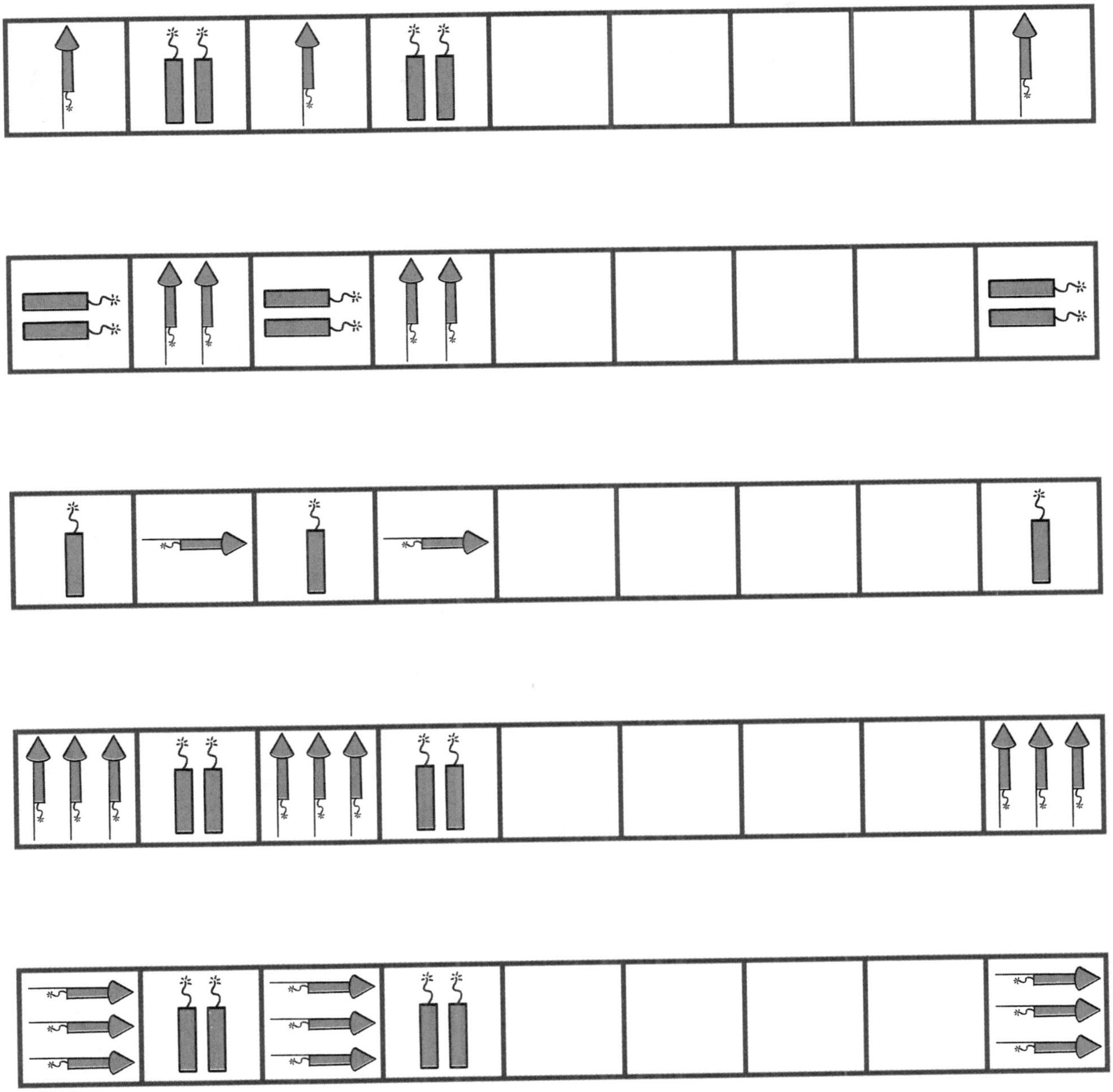

Directions: Have your child study the patterns in each row, then complete the patterns by filling in the spaces with the correct objects. ***Skill:*** Identifying and completing patterns.

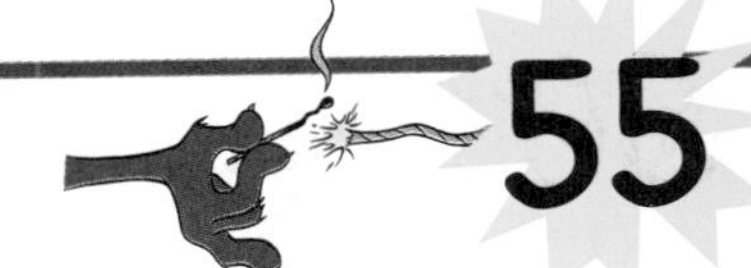

NAME ________________________________

PATTERNS

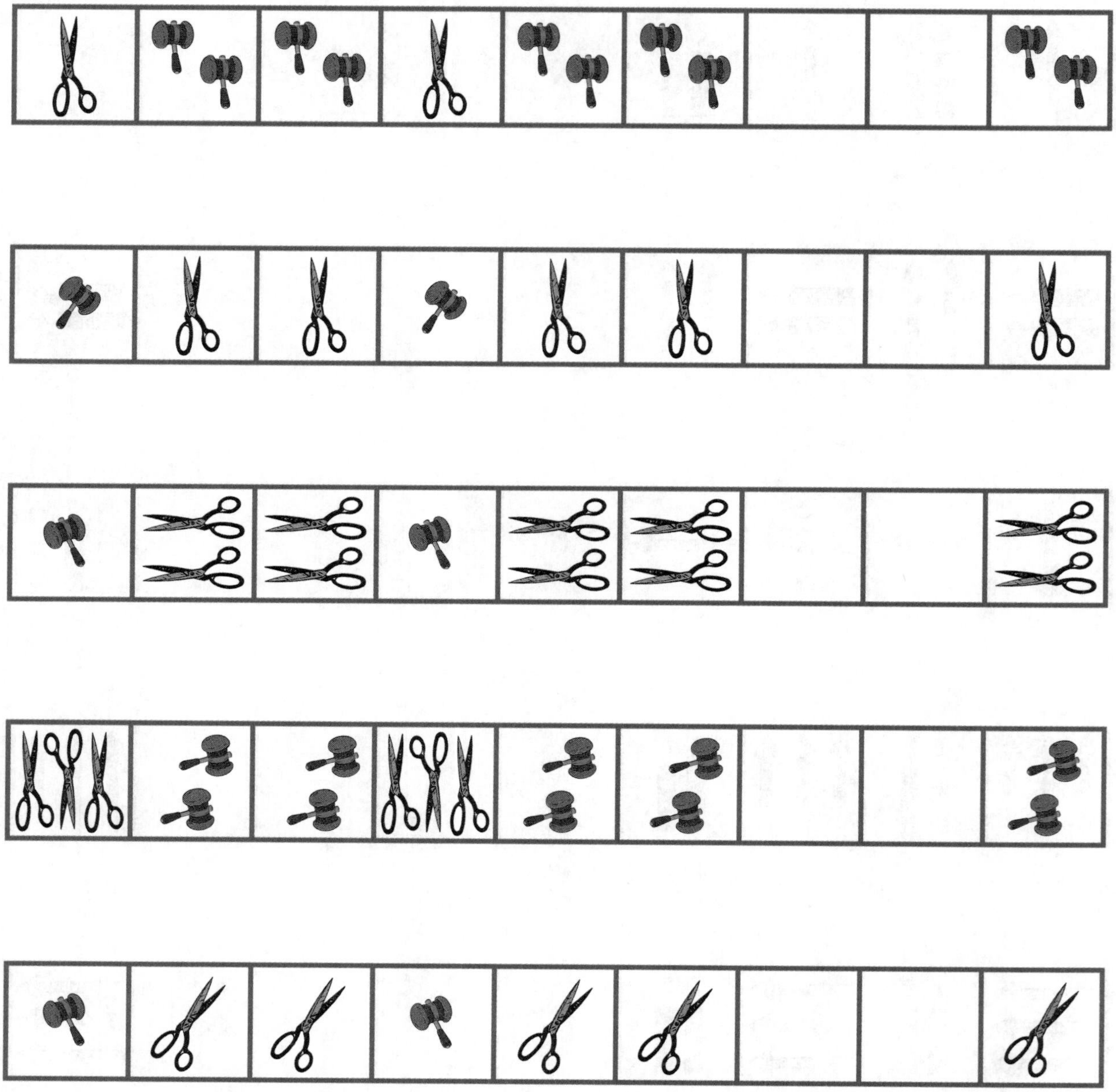

Directions: Have your child study the patterns in each row, then complete the patterns by filling in the spaces with the correct objects. ***Skill:*** Identifying and completing patterns.

NAME ____________________

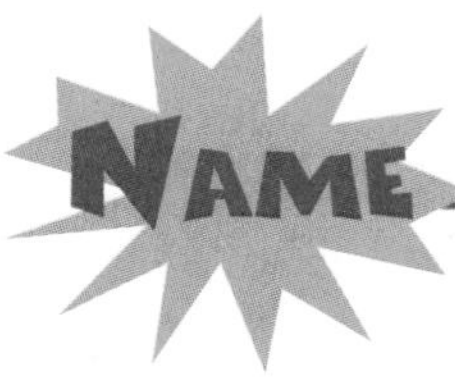

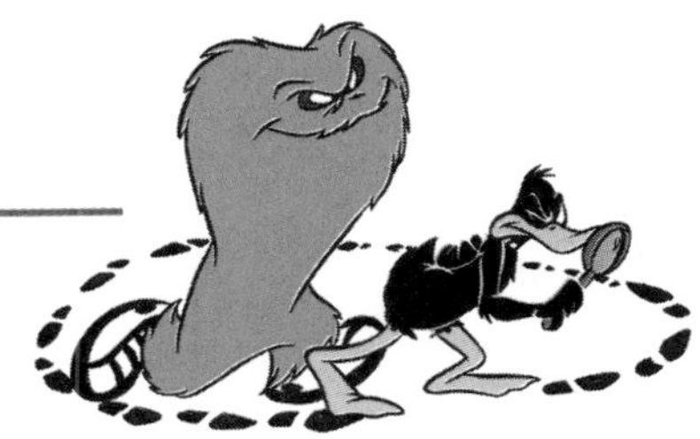

PATTERNS

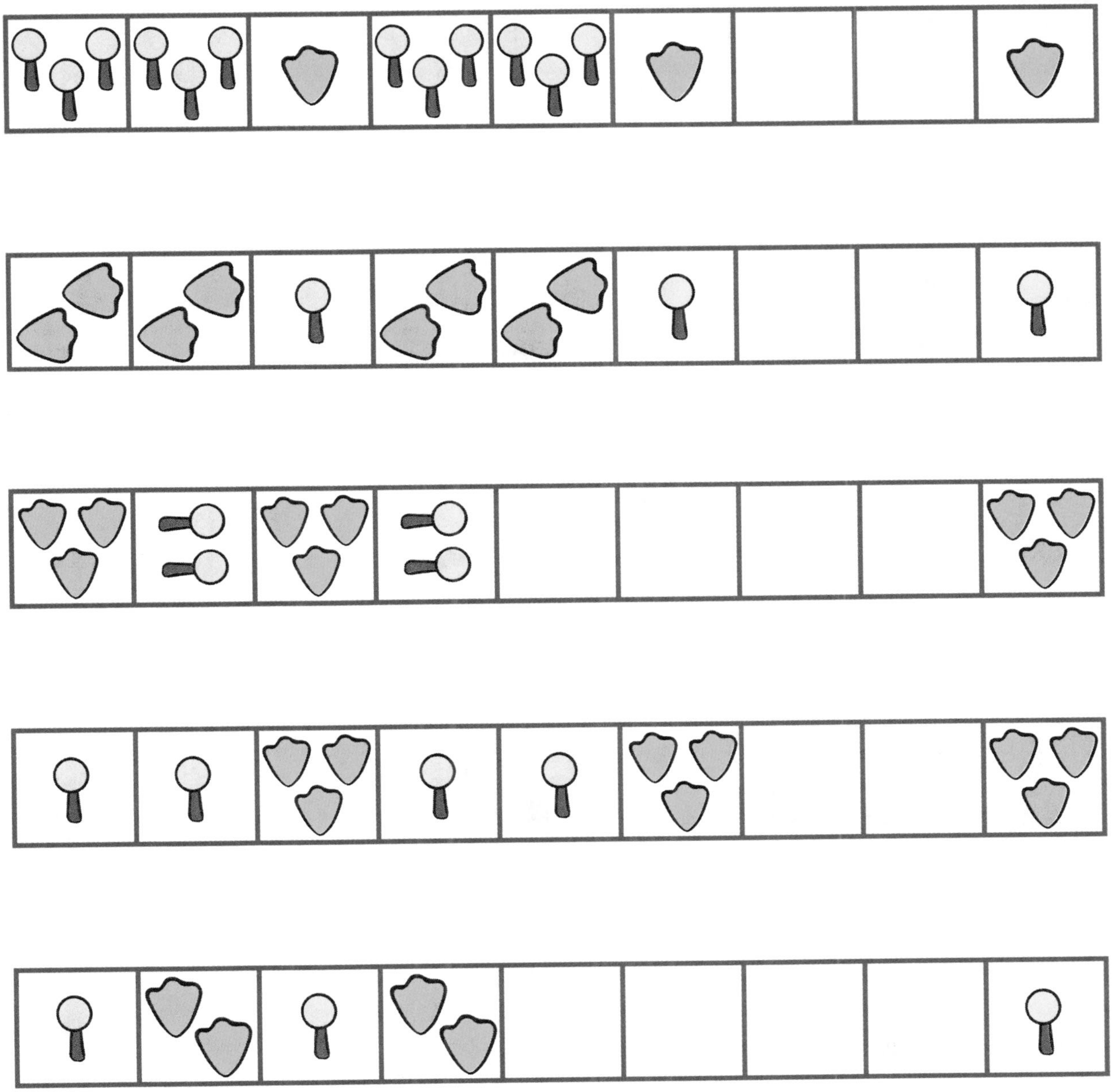

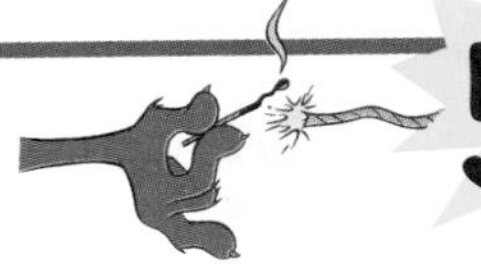

Directions: Have your child study the patterns in each row, then complete the patterns by filling in the spaces with the correct objects. ***Skill:*** Identifying and completing patterns.

NAME

PATTERNS

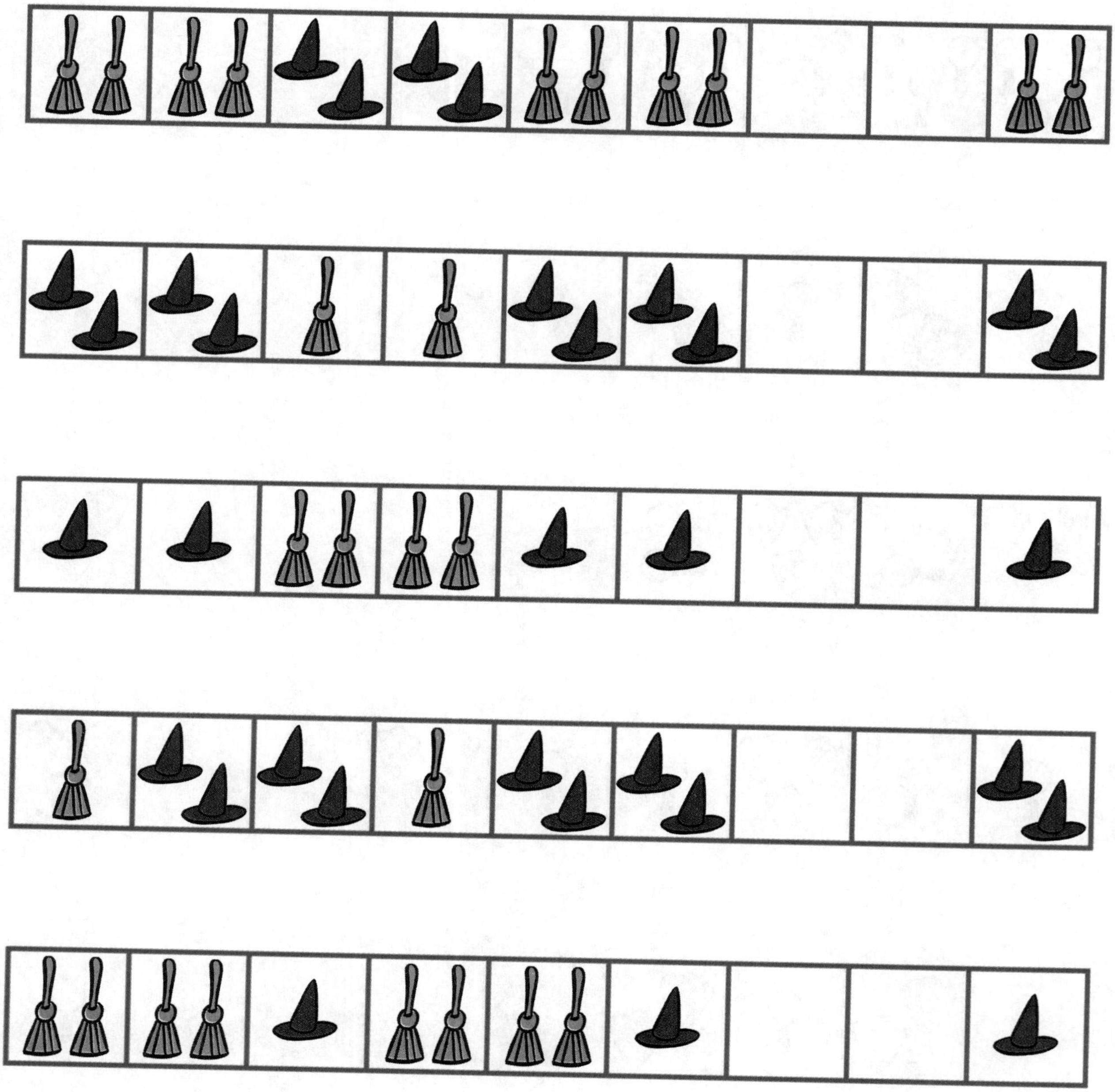

Directions: Have your child study the patterns in each row, then complete the patterns by filling in the spaces with the correct objects. ***Skill:*** Identifying and completing patterns.

Directions: Have your child study the patterns in each row, then complete the patterns by filling in the spaces with the correct colors. ***Skill:*** Identifying and completing patterns.

NAME ___________________________

PATTERNS

Directions: Have your child create original patterns. ***Skill:*** Creating a pattern.

PATTERNS

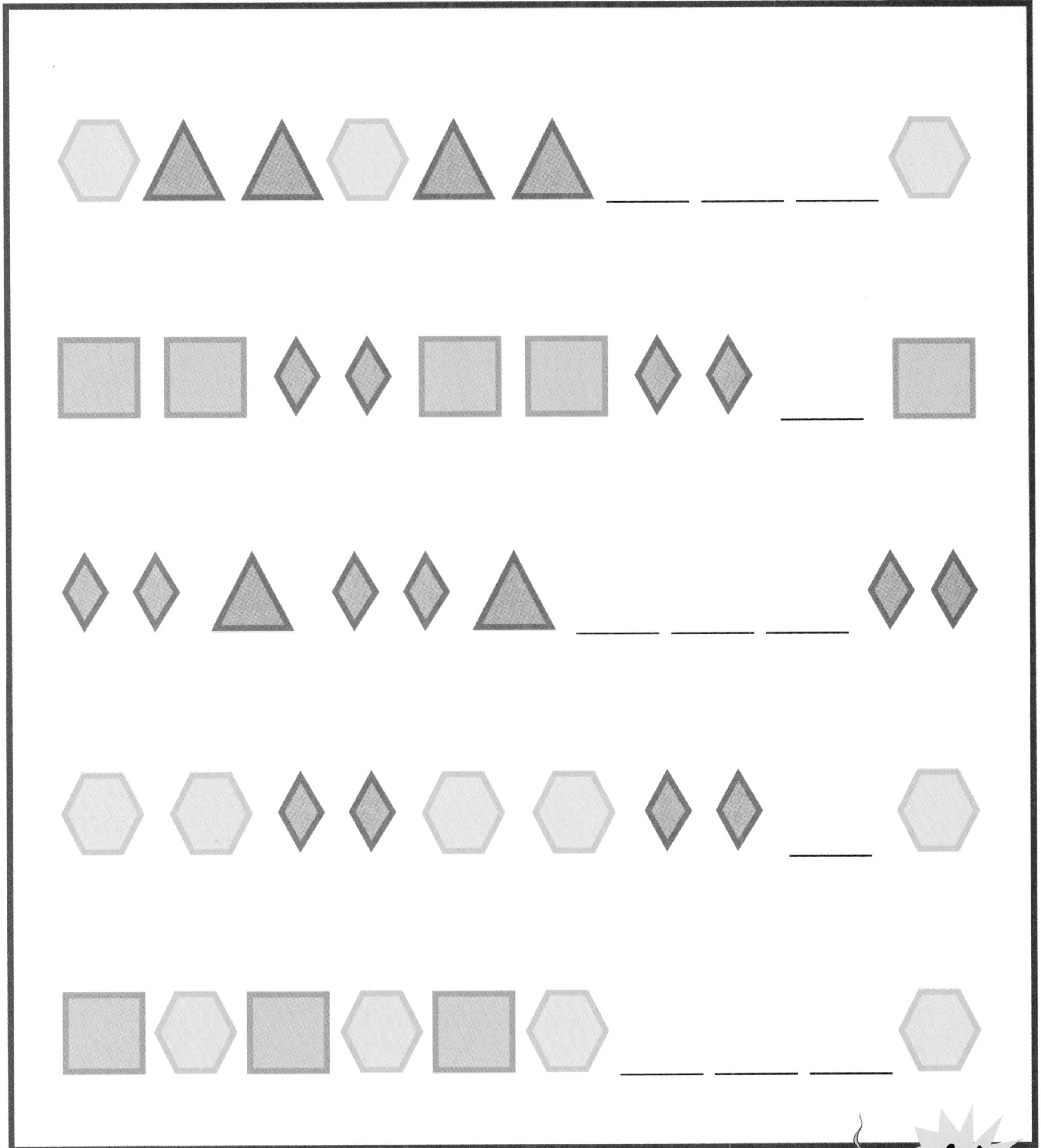

Directions: Have your child study the patterns in each row, then complete the patterns by filling in the spaces with the correct shapes. ***Skill:*** Identifying and completing patterns.

NAME

PATTERNS

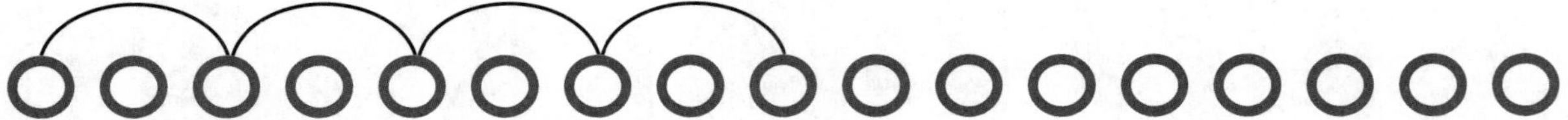

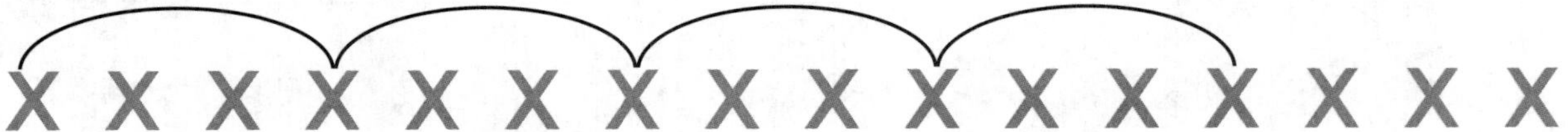

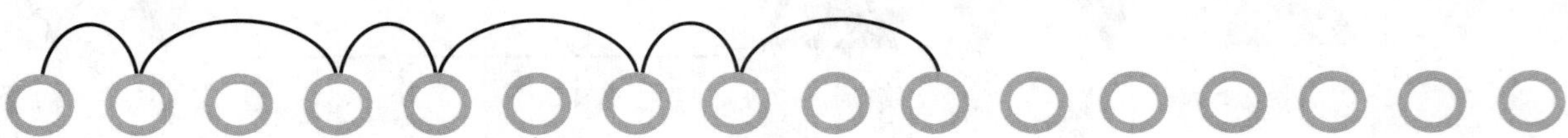

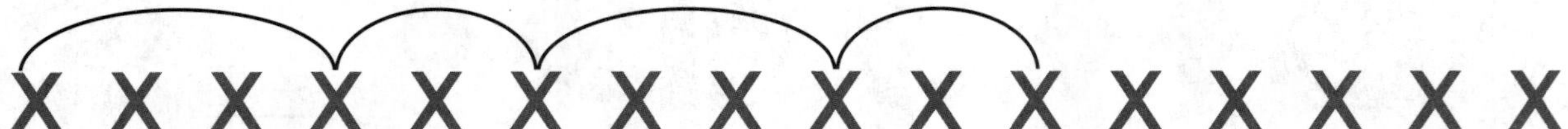

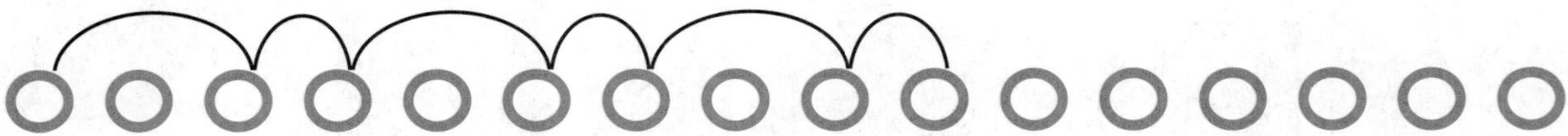

Directions: Have your child study the patterns in each row, then complete the patterns by continuing the line. ***Skill:*** Identifying and completing patterns.

MORE PATTERNS

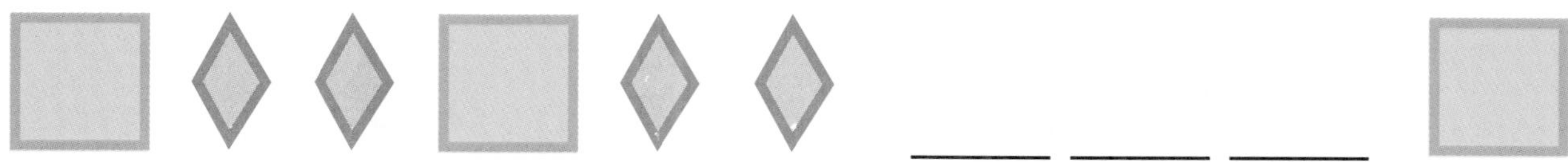

Directions: Have your child study the patterns in each row, then complete the patterns by filling in the spaces with the correct shapes. ***Skill:*** Identifying and completing patterns.

NAME ____________________

MORE PATTERNS

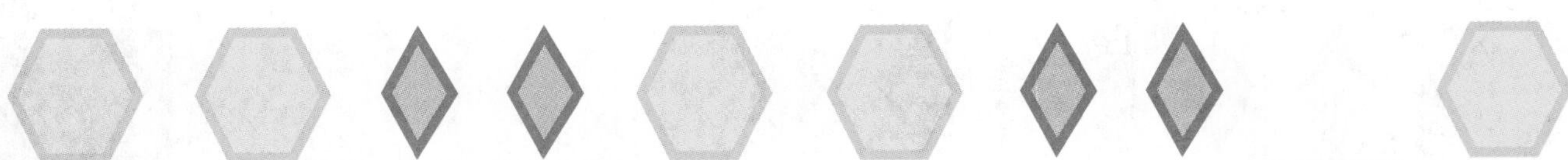

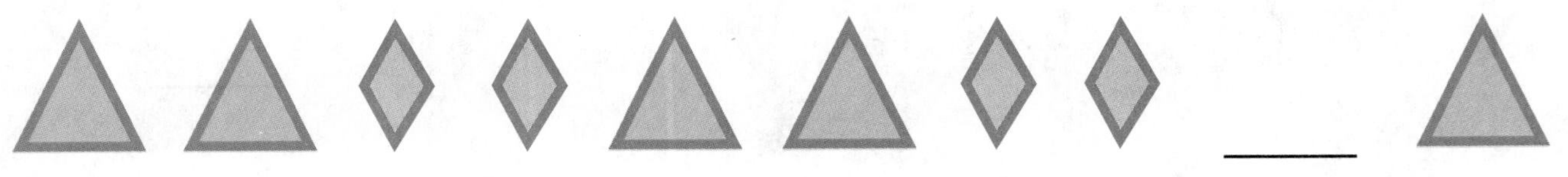

Directions: Have your child study the patterns in each row, then complete the patterns by filling in the spaces with the correct shapes. ***Skill:*** Identifying and completing patterns.

Answer Key

Name

One and Two

Red 2	Brown 1
Brown 1	Red 2
Red 2	Brown 1

Directions: Following the example in the first box, have your child draw scoops of ice cream on each cone to show how many. Then ask your child to color the cones with 1 scoop brown and the cones with 2 scoops red. **Skill:** Identifying one and two.

3

Name

Writing 1 and 2

1 1 1 1

2 2 2 2

2	1
1	2

Directions: Have your child trace, then write the numbers 1 and 2 in the space provided at the top of the page. Ask your child to count the insects in each block, then write 1 or 2 to tell how many. **Skill:** Identifying and writing 1 and 2.

4

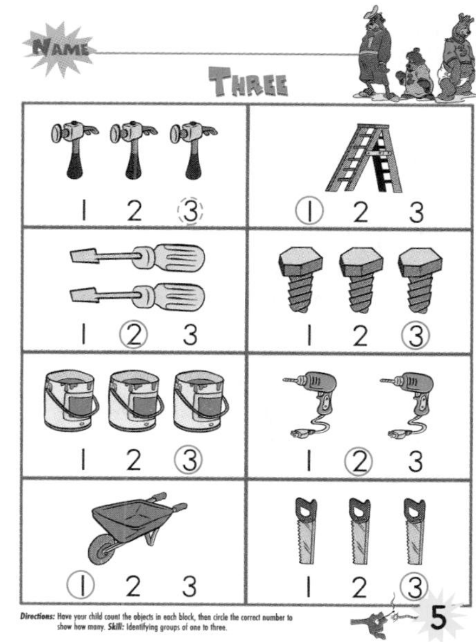

Name

Three

1 2 (3)	(1) 2 3
1 (2) 3	1 2 (3)
1 2 (3)	1 (2) 3
(1) 2 3	1 2 (3)

Directions: Have your child count the objects in each block, then circle the correct number to show how many. **Skill:** Identifying groups of one to three.

5

Name

Four

4	3
2	4
4	1
3	4

Directions: Have your child count the toys in each block, then circle the correct number to show how many. **Skill:** Identifying groups of one to four.

6

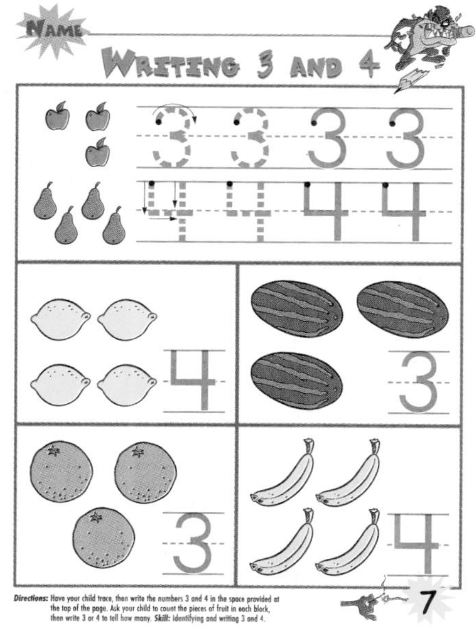

Name

Writing 3 and 4

3 3 3 3

4 4 4 4

4	3
3	4

Directions: Have your child trace, then write the numbers 3 and 4 in the space provided at the top of the page. Ask your child to count the pieces of fruit in each block, then write 3 or 4 to tell how many. **Skill:** Identifying and writing 3 and 4.

7

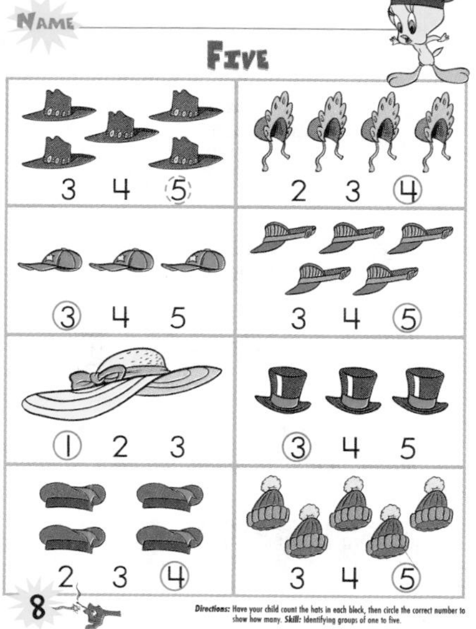

Name

Five

3 4 (5)	2 3 (4)
(3) 4 5	3 4 (5)
(1) 2 3	(3) 4 5
2 3 (4)	3 4 (5)

Directions: Have your child count the hats in each block, then circle the correct number to show how many. **Skill:** Identifying groups of one to five.

8

Answer Key

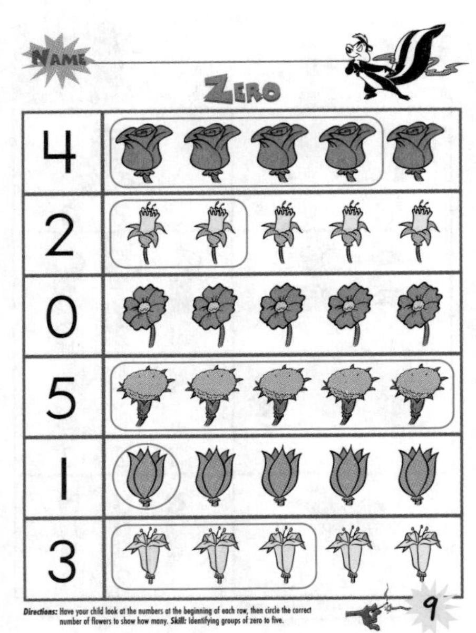
Name
Zero
4
2
0
5
1
3
Directions: Have your child look at the numbers at the beginning of each row, then circle the correct number of flowers to show how many. Skill: Identifying groups of zero to five.
9

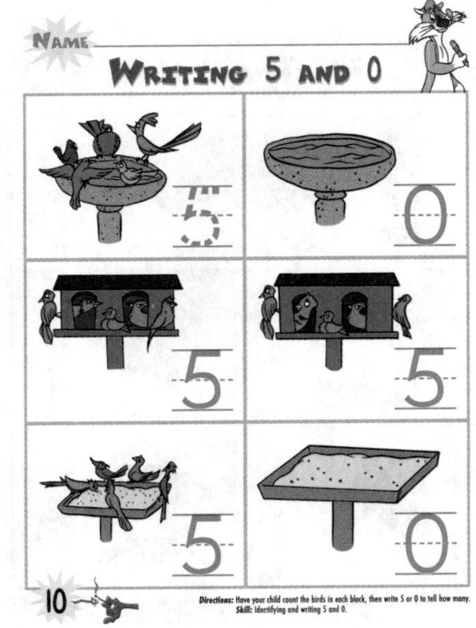
Name
Writing 5 and 0
5
0
5
5
5
0
10
Directions: Have your child count the birds in each block, then write 5 or 0 to tell how many. Skill: Identifying and writing 5 and 0.

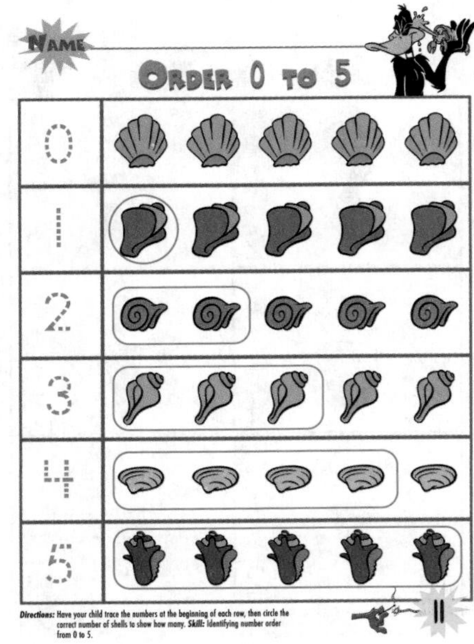
Name
Order 0 to 5
0
1
2
3
4
5
Directions: Have your child trace the numbers at the beginning of each row, then circle the correct number of shells to show how many. Skill: Identifying number order from 0 to 5.
11

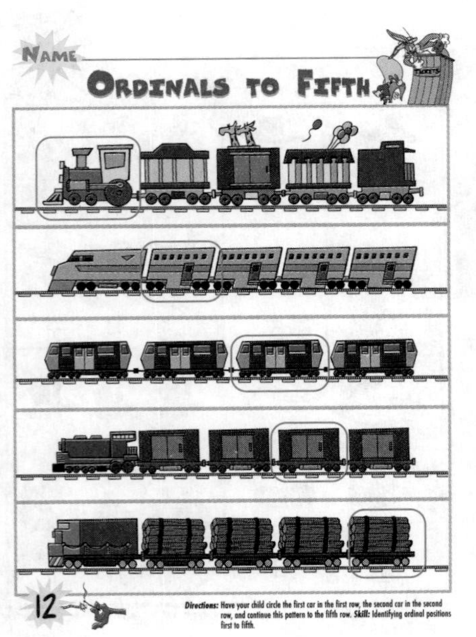
Name
Ordinals to Fifth
12
Directions: Have your child circle the first car in the first row, the second car in the second row, and continue this pattern to the fifth row. Skill: Identifying ordinal positions first to fifth.

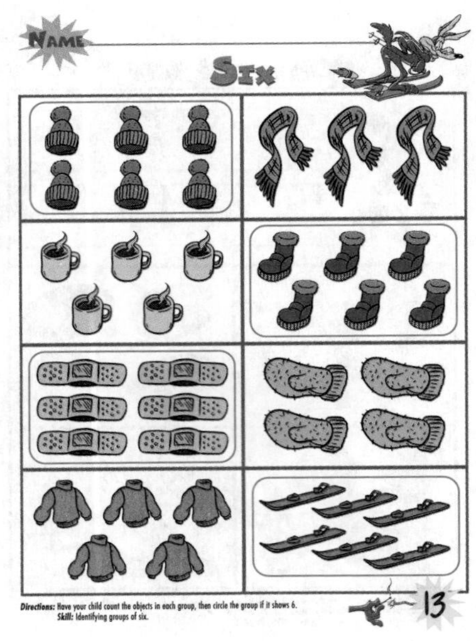
Name
Six
Directions: Have your child count the objects in each group, then circle the group if it shows 6. Skill: Identifying groups of six.
13

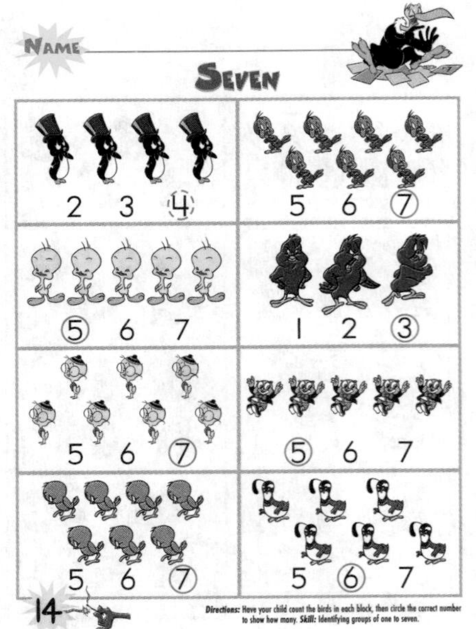
Name
Seven
2 3 4
5 6 7
5 6 7
1 2 3
5 6 7
5 6 7
5 6 7
5 6 7
14
Directions: Have your child count the birds in each block, then circle the correct number to show how many. Skill: Identifying groups of one to seven.

Answer Key

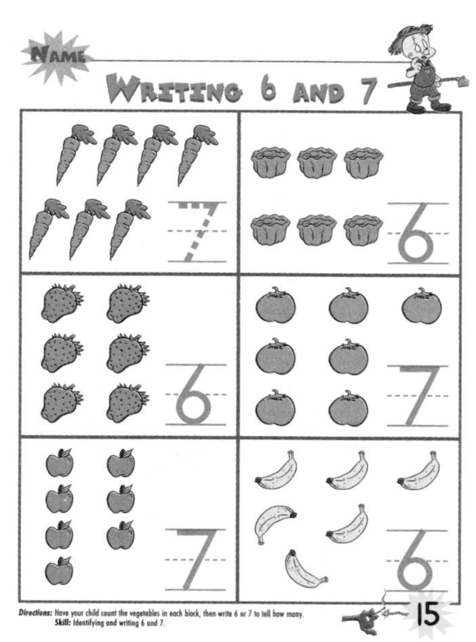
NAME
WRITING 6 AND 7
7
6
6
7
7
6
Directions: Have your child count the vegetables in each block, then write 6 or 7 to tell how many.
Skill: Identifying and writing 6 and 7.
15

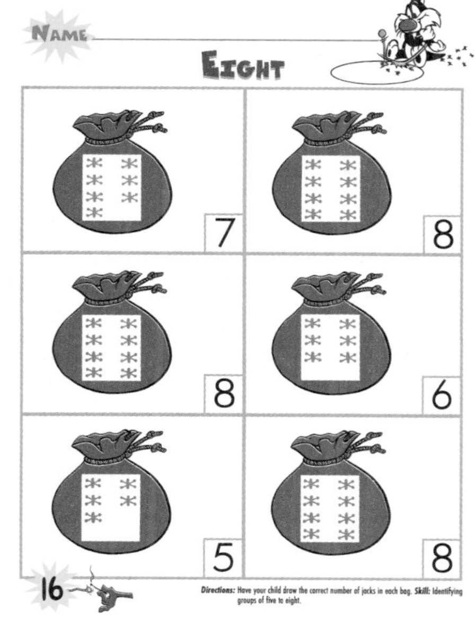
NAME
EIGHT
7
8
8
6
5
8
16
Directions: Have your child draw the correct number of jacks in each bag. Skill: Identifying groups of five to eight.

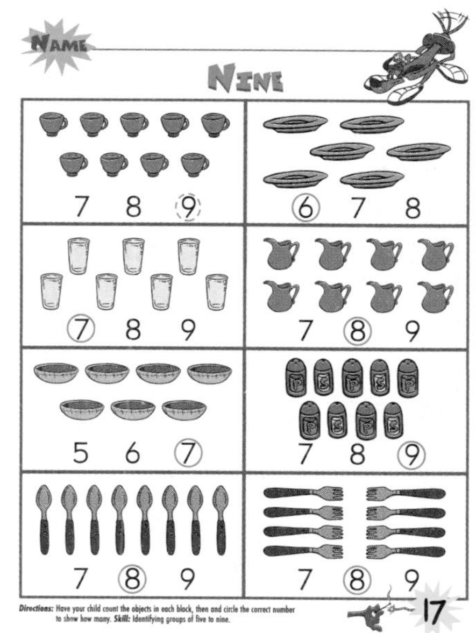
NAME
NINE
7 8 9
6 7 8
7 8 9
7 8 9
5 6 7
7 8 9
7 8 9
7 8 9
Directions: Have your child count the objects in each block, then and circle the correct number to show how many. Skill: Identifying groups of five to nine.
17

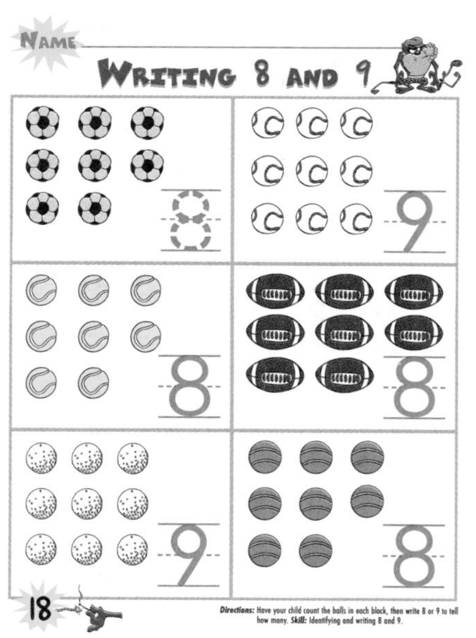
NAME
WRITING 8 AND 9
8
9
8
8
9
8
18
Directions: Have your child count the balls in each block, then write 8 or 9 to tell how many. Skill: Identifying and writing 8 and 9.

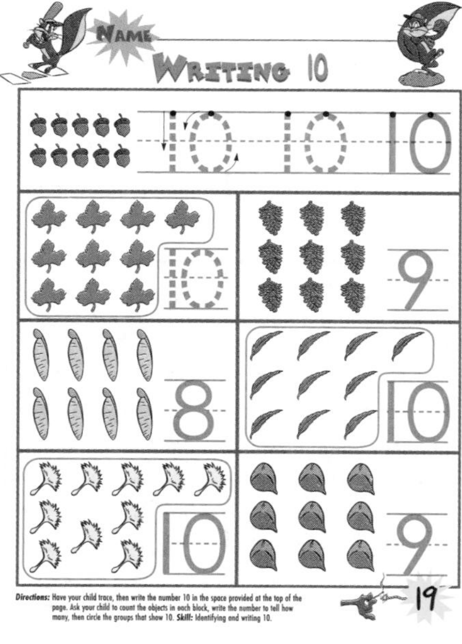
NAME
WRITING 10
10 10 10
10
9
8
10
10
9
Directions: Have your child trace, then write the number 10 in the space provided at the top of the page. Ask your child to count the objects in each block, write the number to tell how many, then circle the groups that show 10. Skill: Identifying and writing 10.
19

NAME
ORDER 0 TO 10
WANTED
0 1 2 3
4 5 6 7
8 9 10
20
Directions: Have your child count the holes in each poster, then write the numbers in the space provided. Skill: Identifying number order and writing 0 to 10.

Answer Key

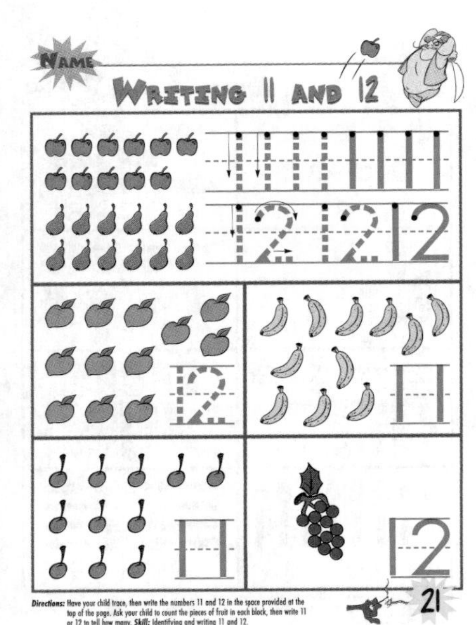

Name

Writing 11 and 12

11 11 11

12 12 12

12 11

11 12

Directions: Have your child trace, then write the numbers 11 and 12 in the space provided at the top of the page. Ask your child to count the pieces of fruit in each block, then write 11 or 12 to tell how many. ***Skill:*** Identifying and writing 11 and 12.

21

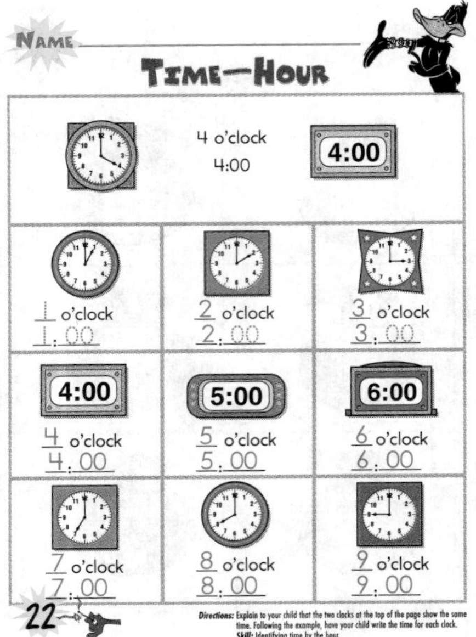

Name

Time—Hour

4 o'clock
4:00

4:00

1 o'clock
1:00

2 o'clock
2:00

3 o'clock
3:00

4:00
4 o'clock
4:00

5:00
5 o'clock
5:00

6:00
6 o'clock
6:00

7 o'clock
7:00

8 o'clock
8:00

9 o'clock
9:00

22

Directions: Explain to your child that the two clocks at the top of the page show the same time. Following the example, have your child write the time for each clock. ***Skill:*** Identifying time by the hour.

Name

Time—Hour

Show this time on this clock.

9:00

Show this time on this clock.

10:00

12:00

11:00

5:00

6:00

2:00

7:00

Directions: Following the example at the top of the page, have your child write the time for each clock. ***Skill:*** Identifying time by the hour.

23

Name

Time—Half Hour

1 o'clock
1:00

one thirty
1:30

2 o'clock
2:00

two thirty
2:30

three thirty
3:30

four thirty
4:30

11:30
eleven thirty
11:30

12:30
twelve thirty
12:30

5:30
five thirty
5:30

six thirty
6:30

ten thirty
10:30

eight thirty
8:30

24

Directions: Explain to your child the time that is shown on each clock at the top of the page. Following the example, have your child write the time for each clock. ***Skill:*** Identifying time by the half-hour.

Name

Time—Half Hour

Show this time on this clock.

11:30

Show this time on this clock.

12:30

12:30

9:30

6:30

10:30

5:30

7:30

Directions: Following the example at the top of the page, have your child write the time for each clock. ***Skill:*** Identifying time by the half-hour.

25

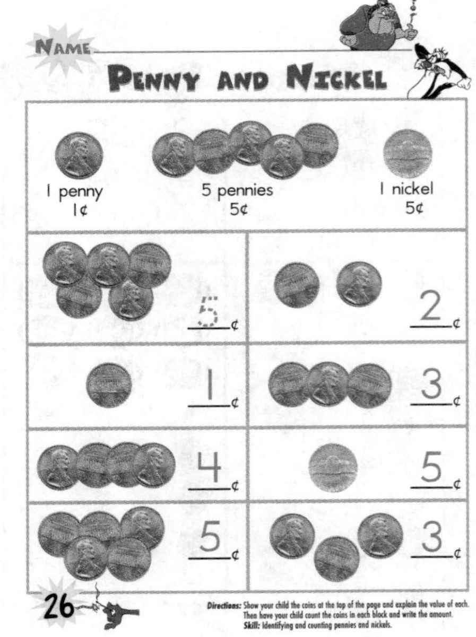

Name

Penny and Nickel

1 penny
1¢

5 pennies
5¢

1 nickel
5¢

5¢

2¢

1¢

3¢

4¢

5¢

5¢

3¢

26

Directions: Show your child the coins at the top of the page and explain the value of each. Then have your child count the coins in each block and write the amount. ***Skill:*** Identifying and counting pennies and nickels.

ANSWER KEY

NAME

PENNY, NICKEL AND DIME

1 penny 1¢ | 1 nickel 5¢ | 1 dime 10¢

10¢	6¢
6¢	8¢
10¢	5¢
10¢	9¢

Directions: Have your child look at the coins at the top of the page and explain the value of each. Then have your child count the coins in each block and write the amount. **Skill:** Identifying and counting pennies, nickels and dimes.

27

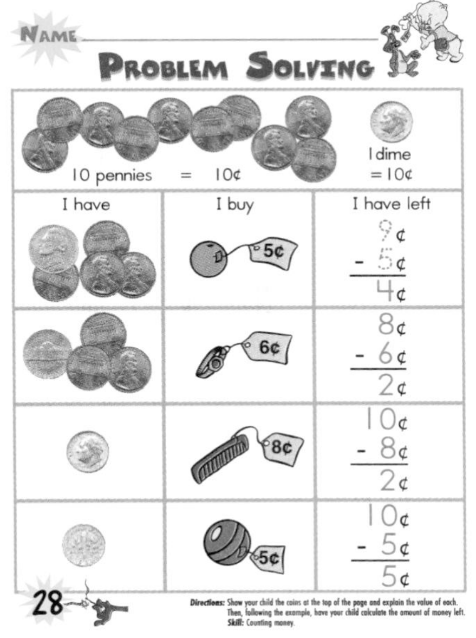
NAME

PROBLEM SOLVING

10 pennies = 10¢ | 1 dime = 10¢

I have	I buy	I have left
	5¢	9¢ - 5¢ = 4¢
	6¢	8¢ - 6¢ = 2¢
	8¢	10¢ - 8¢ = 2¢
	5¢	10¢ - 5¢ = 5¢

28

Directions: Show your child the coins at the top of the page and explain the value of each. Then, following the example, have your child calculate the amount of money left. **Skill:** Counting money.

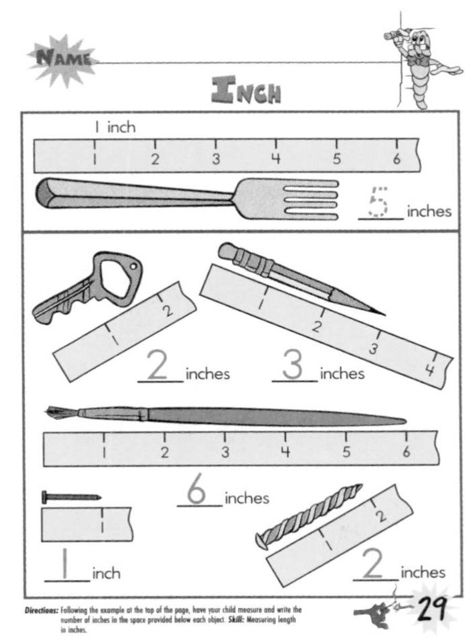
NAME

INCH

Directions: Following the example at the top of the page, have your child measure and write the number of inches in the space provided below each object. **Skill:** Measuring length in inches.

29

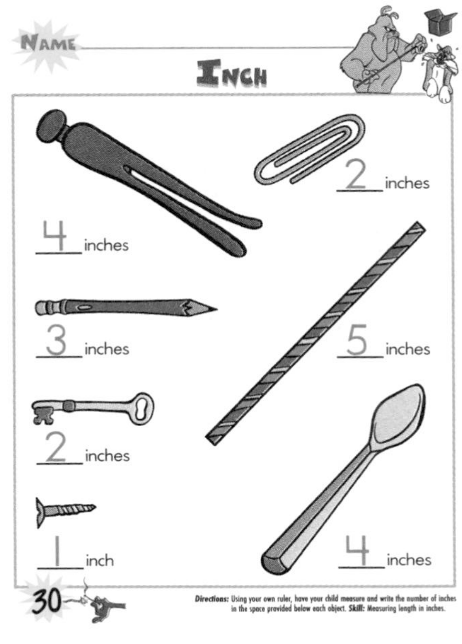
NAME

INCH

30

Directions: Using your own ruler, have your child measure and write the number of inches in the space provided below each object. **Skill:** Measuring length in inches.

NAME

CIRCLE

Directions: Have your child look at the pictures, then place an X on each object that has the shape of a circle. **Skill:** Identifying a circle.

31

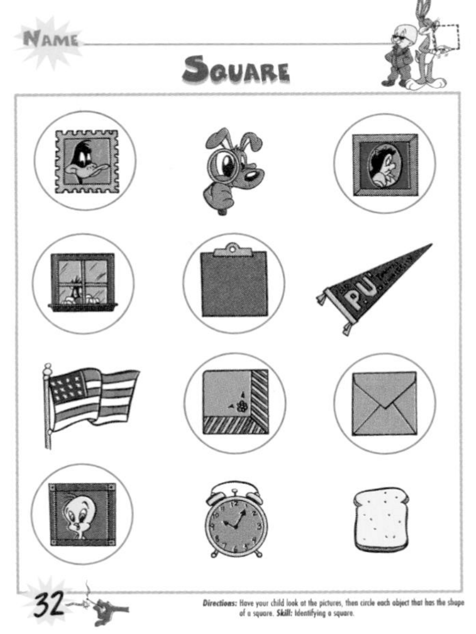
NAME

SQUARE

32

Directions: Have your child look at the pictures, then circle each object that has the shape of a square. **Skill:** Identifying a square.

ANSWER KEY

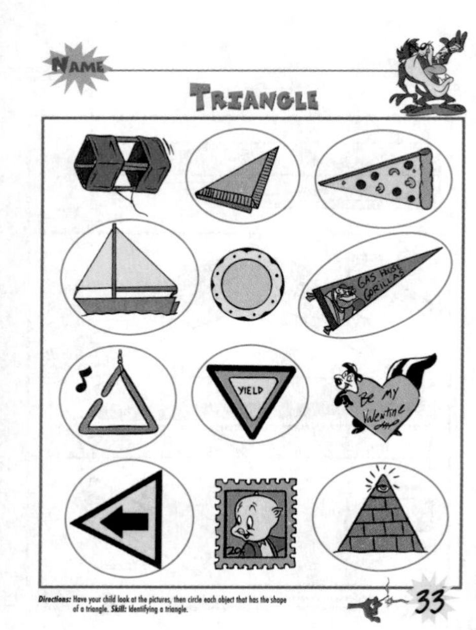
NAME
TRIANGLE
YIELD
Be my Valentine
33
Directions: Have your child look at the pictures, then circle each object that has the shape of a triangle. Skill: Identifying a triangle.

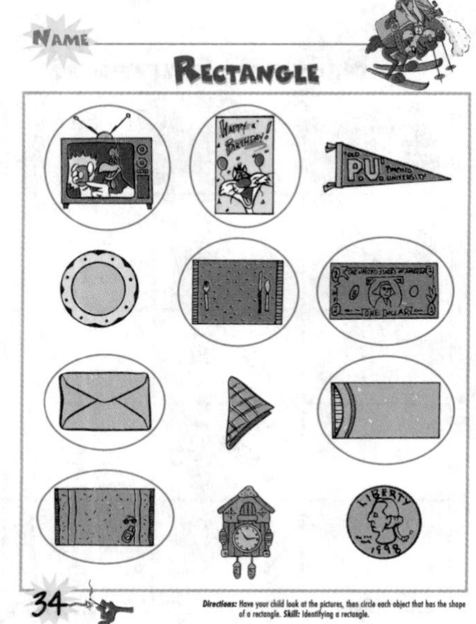
NAME
RECTANGLE
LIBERTY
1998
34
Directions: Have your child look at the pictures, then circle each object that has the shape of a rectangle. Skill: Identifying a rectangle.

NAME
COUNTING AND MATCHING
35
Directions: Have your child count the objects in each block on the left, then draw a line to the block on the right that has the same number of objects. Skill: Counting and matching objects.

NAME
COUNTING AND MATCHING
36
Directions: Have your child count the objects in each block on the left, then draw a line to the block on the right that has the same number of objects. Skill: Counting and matching objects.

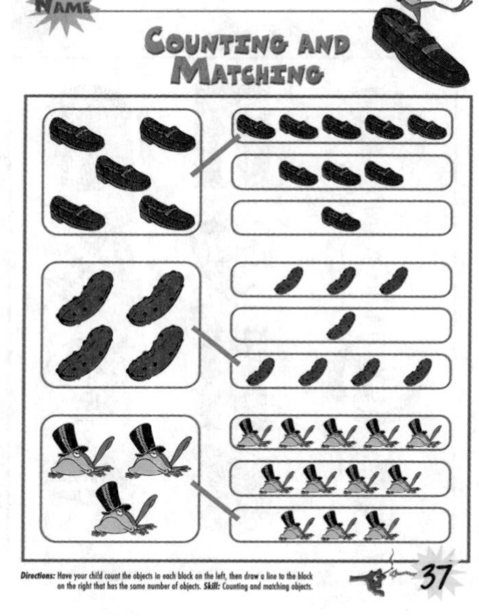
NAME
COUNTING AND MATCHING
37
Directions: Have your child count the objects in each block on the left, then draw a line to the block on the right that has the same number of objects. Skill: Counting and matching objects.

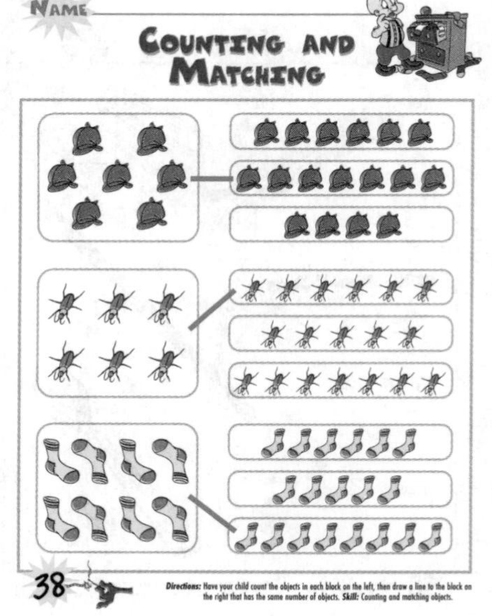
NAME
COUNTING AND MATCHING
38
Directions: Have your child count the objects in each block on the left, then draw a line to the block on the right that has the same number of objects. Skill: Counting and matching objects.

ANSWER KEY

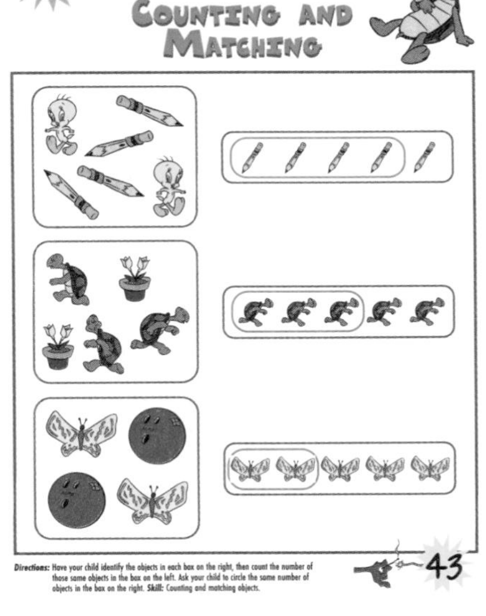

Answer Key

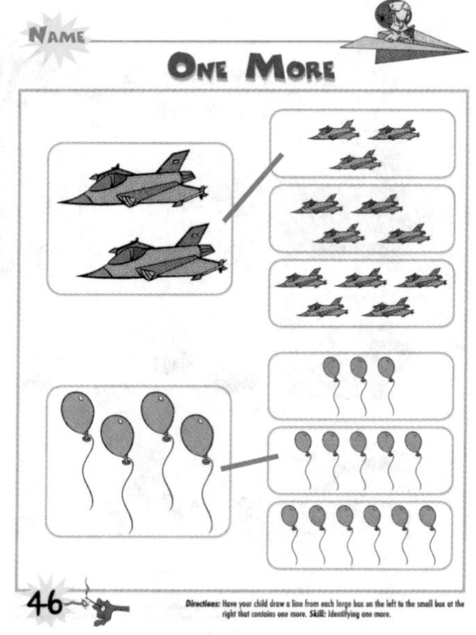

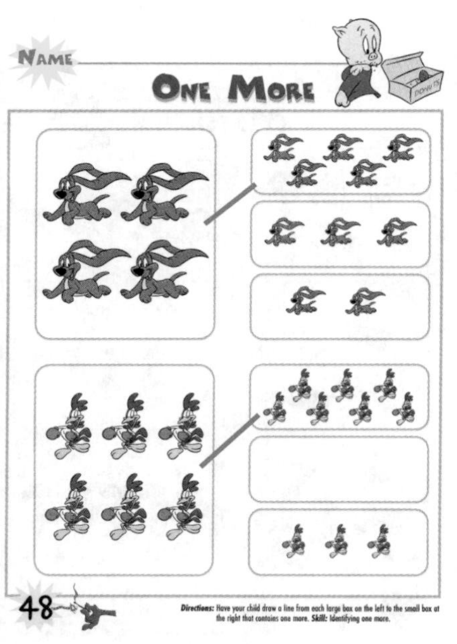
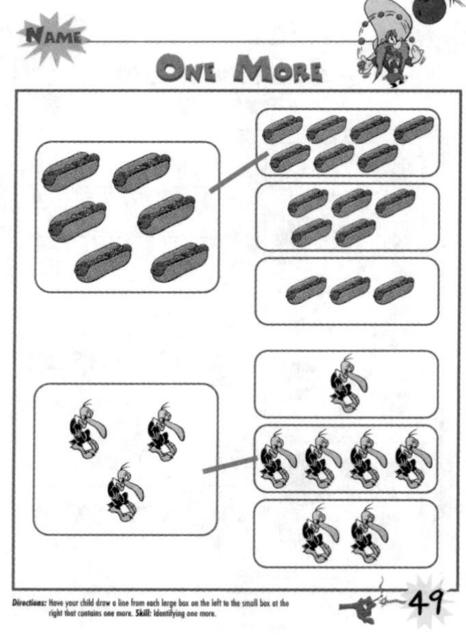

Answer Key

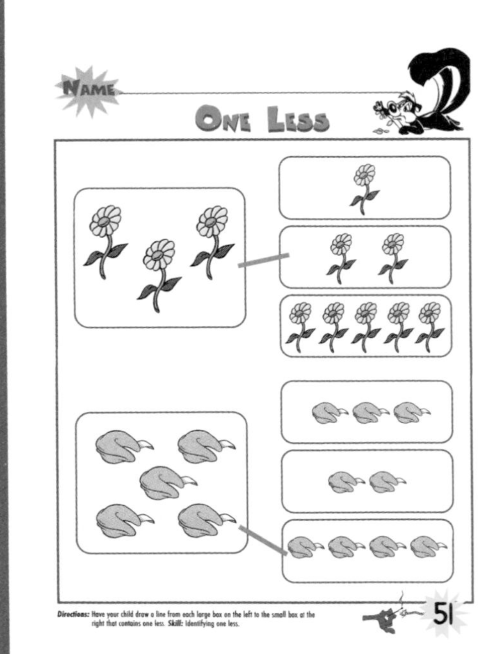

Name
One Less
Directions: Have your child draw a line from each large box on the left to the small box at the right that contains one less. Skill: Identifying one less.
51

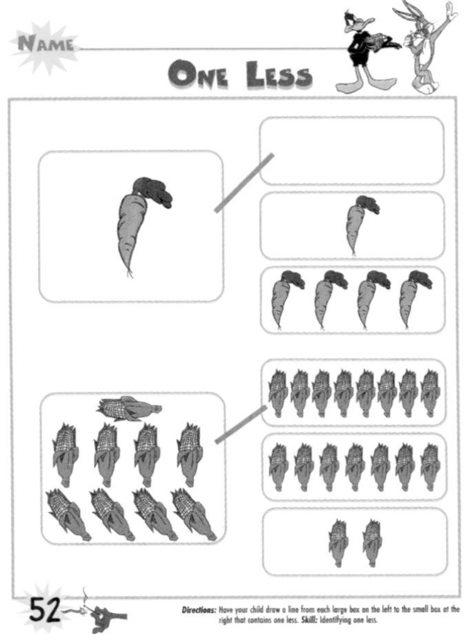

Name
One Less
52
Directions: Have your child draw a line from each large box on the left to the small box at the right that contains one less. Skill: Identifying one less.

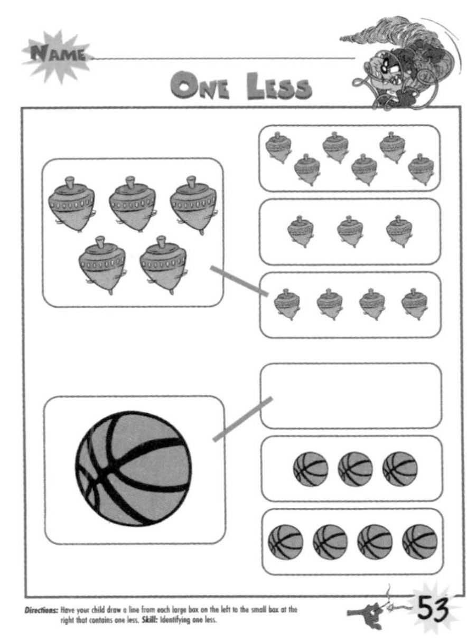

Name
One Less
Directions: Have your child draw a line from each large box on the left to the small box at the right that contains one less. Skill: Identifying one less.
53

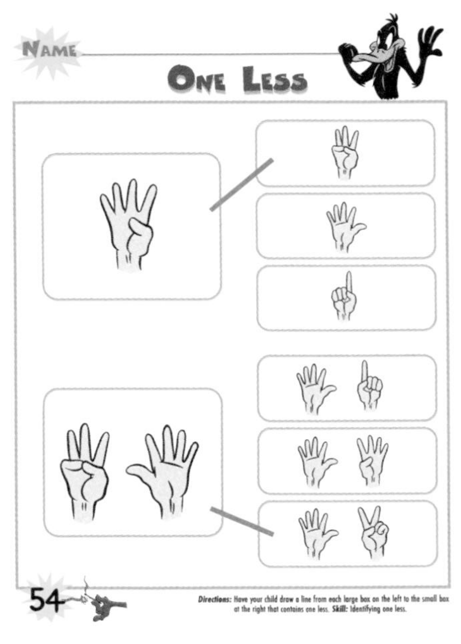

Name
One Less
54
Directions: Have your child draw a line from each large box on the left to the small box at the right that contains one less. Skill: Identifying one less.

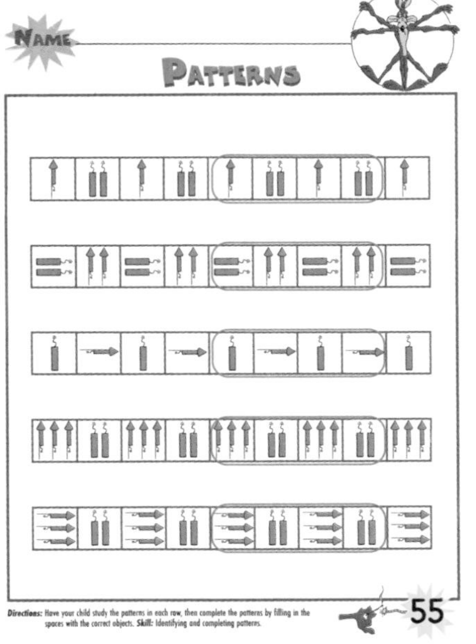

Name
Patterns
Directions: Have your child study the patterns in each row, then complete the patterns by filling in the spaces with the correct objects. Skill: Identifying and completing patterns.
55

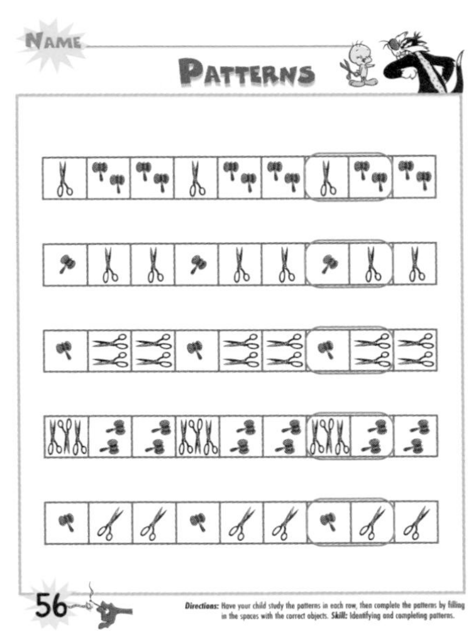

Name
Patterns
56
Directions: Have your child study the patterns in each row, then complete the patterns by filling in the spaces with the correct objects. Skill: Identifying and completing patterns.

ANSWER KEY

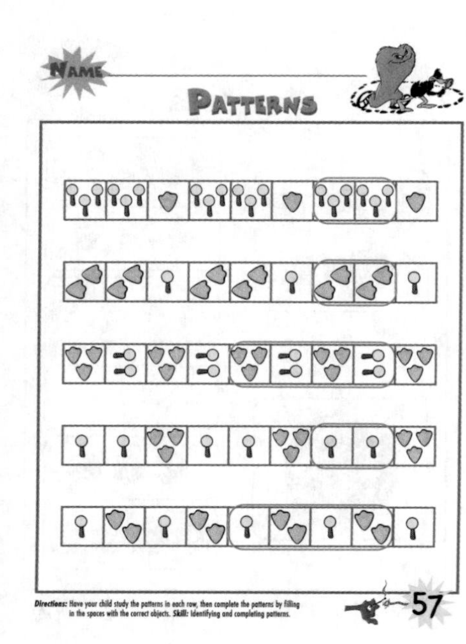
NAME

PATTERNS

Directions: Have your child study the patterns in each row, then complete the patterns by filling in the spaces with the correct objects. ***Skill:*** Identifying and completing patterns.

57

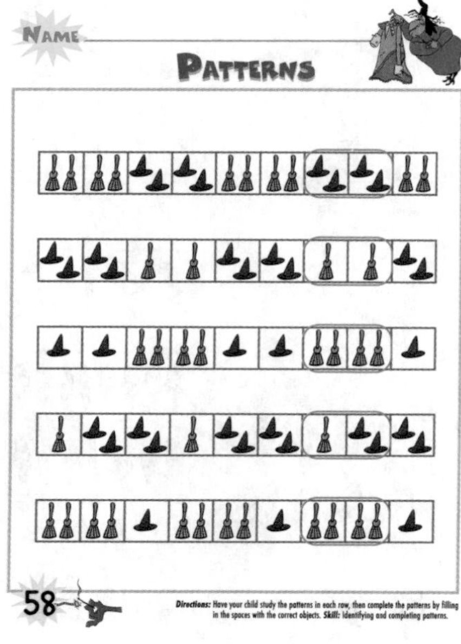
NAME

PATTERNS

58

Directions: Have your child study the patterns in each row, then complete the patterns by filling in the spaces with the correct objects. ***Skill:*** Identifying and completing patterns.

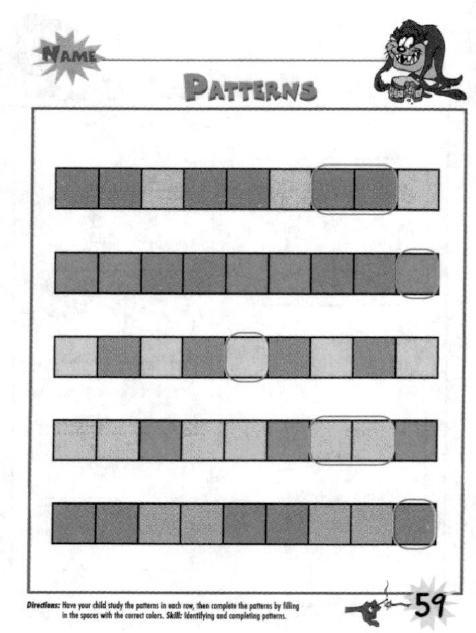
NAME

PATTERNS

Directions: Have your child study the patterns in each row, then complete the patterns by filling in the spaces with the correct colors. ***Skill:*** Identifying and completing patterns.

59

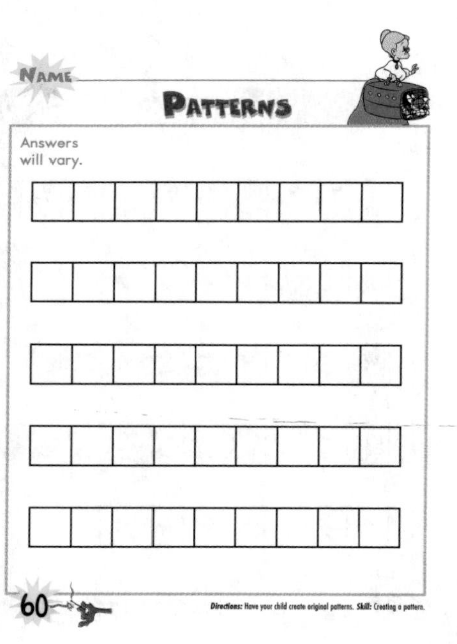
NAME

PATTERNS

Answers will vary.

60

Directions: Have your child create original patterns. ***Skill:*** Creating a pattern.

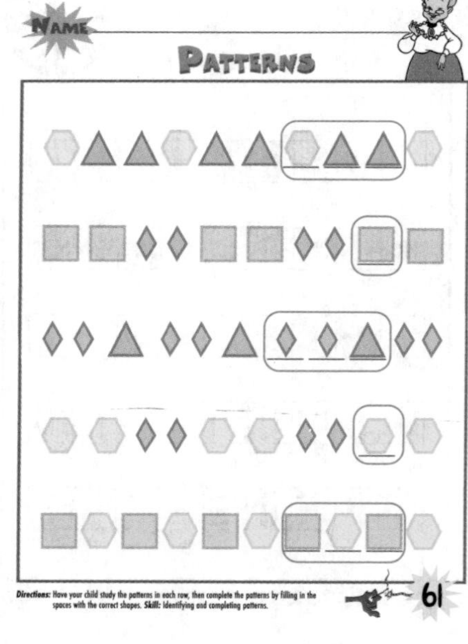
NAME

PATTERNS

Directions: Have your child study the patterns in each row, then complete the patterns by filling in the spaces with the correct shapes. ***Skill:*** Identifying and completing patterns.

61

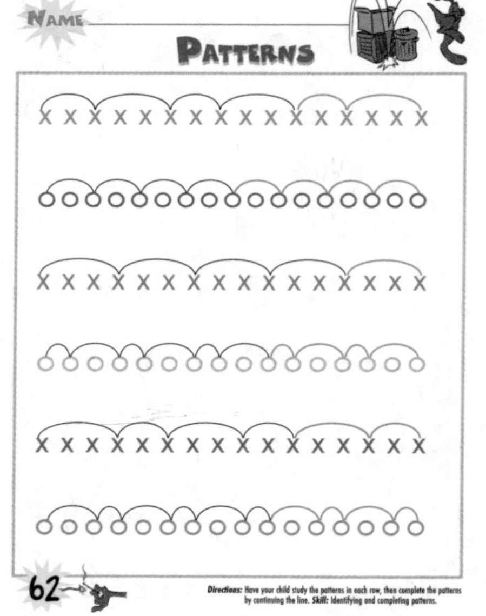
NAME

PATTERNS

62

Directions: Have your child study the patterns in each row, then complete the patterns by continuing the line. ***Skill:*** Identifying and completing patterns.

Answer Key

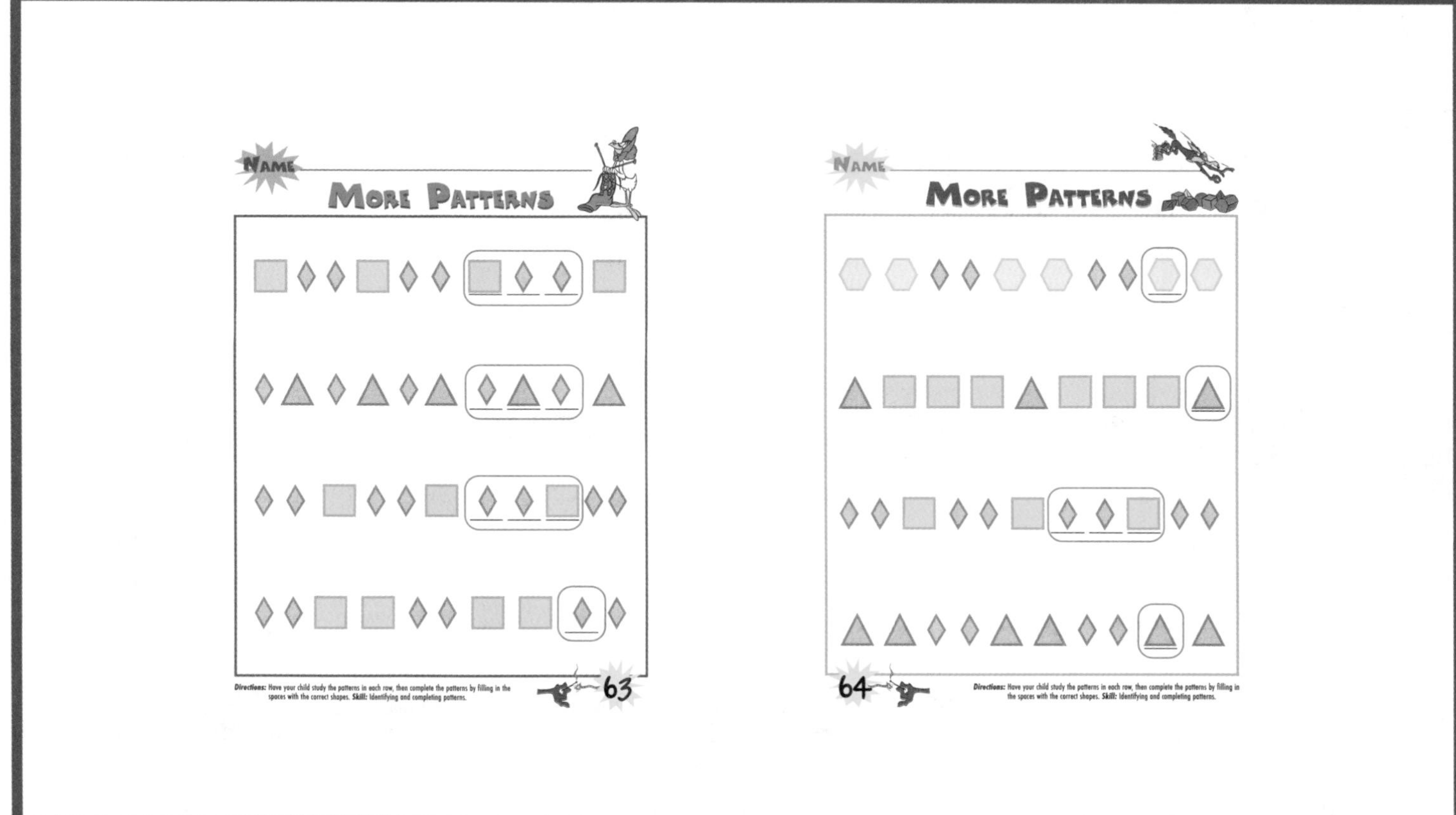

Name
More Patterns
Directions: Have your child study the patterns in each row, then complete the patterns by filling in the spaces with the correct shapes. Skill: Identifying and completing patterns.
63
Name
More Patterns
64
Directions: Have your child study the patterns in each row, then complete the patterns by filling in the spaces with the correct shapes. Skill: Identifying and completing patterns.

Look for all of these entertaining and educational titles in

The McGraw-Hill Junior Academic™ Workbook Series

Toddler

My Colors Go 'Round	ISBN 1-57768-208-4	UPC 6-09746-45118-5
My 1, 2, 3's	ISBN 1-57768-218-1	UPC 6-09746-45128-4
My A, B, C's	ISBN 1-57768-228-9	UPC 6-09746-45138-3
My Ups and Downs	ISBN 1-57768-238-6	UPC 6-09746-45148-2

Preschool

MATH	ISBN 1-57768-209-2	UPC 6-09746-45119-2
READING	ISBN 1-57768-219-X	UPC 6-09746-45129-1
VOWEL SOUNDS	ISBN 1-57768-229-7	UPC 6-09746-45139-0
SOUND PATTERNS	ISBN 1-57768-239-4	UPC 6-09746-45149-9

Kindergarten

MATH	ISBN 1-57768-200-9	UPC 6-09746-45110-9
READING	ISBN 1-57768-210-6	UPC 6-09746-45120-8
PHONICS	ISBN 1-57768-220-3	UPC 6-09746-45130-7
THINKING SKILLS	ISBN 1-57768-230-0	UPC 6-09746-45140-6

Grade 1

MATH	ISBN 1-57768-201-7	UPC 6-09746-45111-6
READING	ISBN 1-57768-211-4	UPC 6-09746-45121-5
PHONICS	ISBN 1-57768-221-1	UPC 6-09746-45131-4
WORD BUILDERS	ISBN 1-57768-231-9	UPC 6-09746-45141-3

Grade 2

MATH	ISBN 1-57768-202-5	UPC 6-09746-45112-3
READING	ISBN 1-57768-212-2	UPC 6-09746-45122-2
PHONICS	ISBN 1-57768-222-X	UPC 6-09746-45132-1
WORD BUILDERS	ISBN 1-57768-232-7	UPC 6-09746-45142-0

It's Serious Fun!!

Offers a selection of workbooks to meet all your needs.

Look for all of these fine educational workbooks in the McGraw-Hill Learning Materials SPECTRUM Series. All workbooks meet school curriculum guidelines and correspond to The McGraw-Hill Companies classroom textbooks.

SPECTRUM SERIES

GEOGRAPHY

Full-color, three-part lessons strengthen geography knowledge and map reading skills. Focusing on five geographic themes including location, place, human/environmental interaction, movement, and regions. Over 150 pages. Glossary of geographical terms and answer key included.

TITLE	ISBN	PRICE
Grade 3, Communities	1-57768-153-3	$7.95
Grade 4, Regions	1-57768-154-1	$7.95
Grade 5, USA	1-57768-155-X	$7.95
Grade 6, World	1-57768-156-8	$7.95

MATH

Features easy-to-follow instructions that give students a clear path to success. This series has comprehensive coverage of the basic skills, helping children to master math fundamentals. Over 150 pages. Answer key included.

TITLE	ISBN	PRICE
Grade 1	1-57768-111-8	$6.95
Grade 2	1-57768-112-6	$6.95
Grade 3	1-57768-113-4	$6.95
Grade 4	1-57768-114-2	$6.95
Grade 5	1-57768-115-0	$6.95
Grade 6	1-57768-116-9	$6.95
Grade 7	1-57768-117-7	$6.95
Grade 8	1-57768-118-5	$6.95

PHONICS

Provides everything children need to build multiple skills in language. Focusing on phonics, structural analysis, and dictionary skills, this series also offers creative ideas for using phonics and word study skills in other language arts. Over 200 pages. Answer key included.

TITLE	ISBN	PRICE
Grade K	1-57768-120-7	$6.95
Grade 1	1-57768-121-5	$6.95
Grade 2	1-57768-122-3	$6.95
Grade 3	1-57768-123-1	$6.95
Grade 4	1-57768-124-X	$6.95
Grade 5	1-57768-125-8	$6.95
Grade 6	1-57768-126-6	$6.95

READING

This full-color series creates an enjoyable reading environment, even for below-average readers. Each book contains captivating content, colorful characters, and compelling illustrations, so children are eager to find out what happens next. Over 150 pages. Answer key included.

TITLE	ISBN	PRICE
Grade K	1-57768-130-4	$6.95
Grade 1	1-57768-131-2	$6.95
Grade 2	1-57768-132-0	$6.95
Grade 3	1-57768-133-9	$6.95
Grade 4	1-57768-134-7	$6.95
Grade 5	1-57768-135-5	$6.95
Grade 6	1-57768-136-3	$6.95

SPELLING

This full-color series links spelling to reading and writing and increases skills in words and meanings, consonant and vowel spellings, and proofreading practice. Over 200 pages. Speller dictionary and answer key included.

TITLE	ISBN	PRICE
Grade 1	1-57768-161-4	$7.95
Grade 2	1-57768-162-2	$7.95
Grade 3	1-57768-163-0	$7.95
Grade 4	1-57768-164-9	$7.95
Grade 5	1-57768-165-7	$7.95
Grade 6	1-57768-166-5	$7.95

WRITING

Lessons focus on creative and expository writing using clearly stated objectives and pre-writing exercises. Eight essential reading skills are applied. Activities include main idea, sequence, comparison, detail, fact and opinion, cause and effect, and making a point. Over 130 pages. Answer key included.

TITLE	ISBN	PRICE
Grade 1	1-57768-141-X	$6.95
Grade 2	1-57768-142-8	$6.95
Grade 3	1-57768-143-6	$6.95
Grade 4	1-57768-144-4	$6.95
Grade 5	1-57768-145-2	$6.95
Grade 6	1-57768-146-0	$6.95
Grade 7	1-57768-147-9	$6.95
Grade 8	1-57768-148-7	$6.95

TEST PREP from the Nation's #1 Testing Company

Prepares children to do their best on current editions of the five major standardized tests. Activities reinforce test-taking skills through examples, tips, practice, and timed exercises. Subjects include reading, math, and language. Over 150 pages. Answer key included.

TITLE	ISBN	PRICE
Grade 3	1-57768-103-7	$8.95
Grade 4	1-57768-104-5	$8.95
Grade 5	1-57768-105-3	$8.95
Grade 6	1-57768-106-1	$8.95
Grade 7	1-57768-107-X	$8.95
Grade 8	1-57768-108-8	$8.95

A McGraw • Hill/Warner Bros. Workbook

CERTIFICATE OF ACCOMPLISHMENT

THIS CERTIFIES THAT

HAS SUCCESSFULLY COMPLETED
THE JUNIOR ACADEMIC'S™

WORKBOOK.
CONGRATULATIONS AND THAT'S ALL FOLKS!

The McGraw·Hill Companies
PUBLISHER

Bugs Bunny
BUGS BUNNY, EDITOR-IN-CHIEF